Ruling with a Sequined Fist
The Gay Handbook

Ruling with a Sequined Fist
The Gay Handbook

Dan Saniski

To Stefan

Contents

Acknowledgements

It took the support, enthusiasm, and dedication of many people to get this book completed and in your hands. First, I would like to thank Mobius for helping me work out the initial idea over omelets and fizzy water. I was then greatly encouraged by the early enthusiasm of Robbie and Marissa. They helped me believe in this project even before I did. Many thanks to my initial readers of the first draft and blog posts: Dan, Becky, Katie, Justin, and Jace. Many thanks to Dr. Matthew Callahan and my darling Stefan for their close reading of the manuscript and brilliant suggestions. I am very thankful to have Stefan in my life, supporting me each day in my artistic endeavors.

Special thanks to the wonderful town of State College, Pennsylvania and its great gay bar, Chumley's. Many of the concepts in this book were worked out there with friends, acquaintances, and colleagues over quite a few Yuenglings and I am eternally grateful. Of the residents (current and former) of State College, special thanks to Ellen, Mer, Andrew, Michael, Justin, Adam, John, Jason, Jose, Nathan, Love and Light Productions, and The Clitorati for helping me to see the world in different and marvelous ways. Without all of you, I would not have the unique perspectives and good company I've had the immense pleasure of enjoying.

Thanks to The Lavender Library, Archives, and Cultural Exchange of Sacramento, California—especially Ron, Buzz, Clint, and David—for providing such a fabulous collection of LGBT materials. Many thanks to Michelle the Redheaded Ninja for the incredible book cover design. Thanks also to the super-sexy cover model who wishes to remain anonymous, but deserves thanks all the same. Last, but certainly not least, thanks to my mom and dad for raising me and my darling sister Katie for being awesome.

Introduction

Congratulations, Mary, you're gay. Now that you're out, it's time to learn how to become fabulous. If you're having some difficulty becoming the top-notch gay you know you can be, this book is for you. If you have difficulty figuring out the difference between a trick, a lover, and a boyfriend then this book is for you. If you want to embody the critically important four gay social skills: glamour, filth, camp, and divinity, then this book is for you. Even if your whole life is wrapped in gold lamé you can always try a little harder to get an edge on all the other queens.

Greenhorn queers heed this warning: being gay is more than sucking cock. It is being part of a massive, global culture with a unique set of symbols, customs, and people. It is, if you will, a fraternity: The Fraternal Alliance of Gays (F.A.G., if you will). From the minute you come out you are offered a sequined world and it is your responsibility to discover the rules, the customs, and the glory. Maybe you're a muscular jock fond of using the word "bro." You might be a leather enthusiast. Perhaps you're a Dungeons and Dragons player. Or an antiques dealer. Or a farmer in Kansas. No matter what you get into you are fabulous and you know it, but you might not know how to show it. You may be born gay, but being fabulous takes work. Thus: *Ruling with a Sequined Fist.*

This is not the first gay handbook ever written. *The Homosexual Handbook* came out in 1968 and provided practical advice on everything from befriending gays to cock sucking interspersed with bizarre, colorful anecdotes from the author's unusual pre-Stonewall associates. It was lauded by *Variety* because, I kid you not, there were descriptions and locations of gay bars, and these bars *actually existed.* Then, in the early 1980s when an especially fascist gay trend known as "clones" was in full swing the brilliant and witty *Butch Manual* came out. This book detailed the simple décor of a clone: work boots, tight jeans, a small t-shirt, aviator sunglasses, and a bomber jacket. It was sex-positive and silly in all the right ways. As anyone can tell you, things got very bleak during the 80s and then, in the early 1990s, *The Unofficial Gay Manual* was released. Although useful at the time, gay men and gay culture have had ups and downs since then and so much has changed as to make the queer landscape unrecognizable— though the coverage of huge (at the time) circuit parties provides a fantastic historical perspective. The time for Gen X apologist writings where authors needed to pat fresh queens on the back and say: "it's okay to be gay; we're normal people too; we're not all hairdressers and drag queens" has also passed. We live in the twenty-first century with gay cultural idioms that reflect, build upon, and move beyond the needs of prior gays. Some of us want to get married and lead "conventional" lives; others want to be open about being anti-assimilationist freaks. If we're open about the fact that some gays are shockingly normal while others are outré, we will be better equipped to help and understand one another. Since both the ultimate centrist and the outrageous non-conformist are lumped into the same broad culture, there is a need for generalized rules applicable to all queers.

Gays, no matter their origins or inclinations, have some common perspectives, experiences, and skills. We come out, we date and fuck around a bit, we struggle to find a part of gay society where we feel accepted, and we live our lives. We all learn to tell the difference between gathering friends and lovers (if we find a difference at all) and it's difficult. We project masculine and feminine genders and discover each attracts different people and has its own benefits and drawbacks. There are many experiences common to queer life; the similarities and differences can be subtle. A guidebook helps when you don't know the difference between a trick, a boyfriend, or a best friend, and if one can't tell the difference between types of drag queens or the seemingly incongruous gays on the streets, in the bars, and in the community. There's a learning curve to homosexual life.

Ruling with a Sequined Fist will take you from recently out to fully fabulous and help you gay up where you live, find a gay job, fuck your brains out, maybe settle down, and ultimately become glamour personified. You will learn about the gay social spectrum, the four gay humours, the places to trick, and how to date one or more people. The four gay humours, by the way, are the skills truly critical to queer survival. They are glamour, camp, filth, and divinity. We'll get into the details soon, my dear.

Before attempting to master faggotry remember that gay society and culture, while it has very stable stereotypical tropes, is not homogenous by any means. There are groupings and stereotypes and they appear now and again throughout the book for illustrative purposes. Gays populate the cities, the suburbs, the plains, the forests, and all spaces in between. An urbane queer and a backwoods queen lead vastly different lives, but there is plenty of common ground along the way and this book provides the skills to flourish with club kids, at a Midtown cocktail party, or down on the farm at a pig roast.

Although this book assumes the reader has little knowledge of queer culture, it should have material detailed enough to stimulate both the novice and the seasoned queen. Hopefully both groups will find plenty of gems, though someone with passing experience in gay culture will probably have better starting traction. One thing not extensively covered here is coming out. It's a challenging and very, very, very well-documented process so we'll be breezing by it quickly.

This book was extensively researched and many of the social tools and skills detailed were designed and tested in all-gay social circles to great acclaim. I am, however, a product of my own biases. They shaped my experiences in gay life as much as your biases will shape yours. I tried to generalize as much as possible and make the lessons here useful to the classy, the trashy, and everyone in between. Remember: very few of us are raised in gay culture. Our parents don't recount our history and our schools would rather pretend we don't exist. As a result all gay men are amateur anthropologists—assembling skills, opinions, and cultural artifacts allowing them to thrive in a culture wrapped up in the eternal now. In an effort to be as timeless as possible, I saved all direct cultural lists (the books to read, the movies to watch, etc.) until the appendix and focused on the processes that make someone fabulous rather than the current (and eventually to be outdated) fashions and media surrounding us. Fads are highly subject to change, but over time the methods to being an expert at glamour, camp, filth, and divinity have remained fairly constant in gay life. Not everyone thinks a particular look is fabulous and it'll be out of season soon enough.

Some methods and ideas detailed in this book are illegal. They are presented for illustrative purposes only. I would never dare tell nubile young queers to commit crimes, only point out that some people get their kicks outside the law. Please follow the laws in your local jurisdiction.

This book focuses on the gay man's path to glamour and only the gay man's path. Lesbians, trannies, and all the other queers are wonderful and have valid needs and an equally wonderful journey of discovery. Their cultures heavily cross-pollinate with gay men and differ wildly as well. I cannot pretend to understand or document those needs in any meaningful way. For the purposes of this book let's just say we need one another and we all hope to achieve the same goal of leading fulfilled lives, but the paths we take look quite different.

Now that the preliminaries are out of the way, let's begin. We will start with coming out and meeting our first gays—a phase we all go through.

The World Outside the Closet

Figuring Out You're Gay

When you were little you always knew there was something different about you. When the boys in the schoolyard discussed their plans for the little girls, you may have played along, but you were imagining what you'd like to do with your guy-pals. You got excessively excited about games of shirts versus skins. Group showers were exhilarating and terrifying—what if you got a boner?

No matter how idyllic your childhood was, eventually someone called you or someone you knew a faggot. The kids who liked to dance, or had feelings, or were otherwise was just outside of fascist childhood ideals of normal were branded the same way: faggot, sissy, queer. It cut many ways—both because it was such a terribly vicious insult and because you began to understand you were this person everyone feared. The perpetual hatred made it seem so scary to deal with these feelings. "Don't be such a pansy." "Only faggots aren't good at sports." "Only queers like to sing." "That outfit is so gay." If every step out of line from hyper-masculine athleticism devoid of feeling is faggy (and I'm pretty sure I'm one of these people everyone detests), what comes next? The world on the other side of those insults was too terrifying to approach. So you buried those feelings deep inside for days, weeks, months, years, maybe even decades. Clearly no one is one of these horrible people—especially not me!

You tried to fit in, act "masculine," and maybe even dated a few girls. Hopefully, you thought, if you tried hard enough, these feelings will go away. So you ignored the way your best guy-friend made you feel when you spent time together or the stir in your pants when a cute guy smiled at you. You kept fantasizing about these guys no matter how far you tried to push the thoughts away.

Then, finally, one day something snapped. Maybe you meet another guy who seems to have these same strange feelings. Perhaps the exhaustion of pretending to be a false straight guy got too tiring. Maybe you got drunk and had a "let's never speak of this again" night of passion with a friend. It's difficult to put up a continually false front. Eventually the façade starts to crack. The feelings, long repressed, start to come out in your dreams and you fantasize more and more about men and less and less about the "normal" life everyone around you seems to dream of: meeting a nice girl, settling down, and starting a straight family.

Fear follows closely behind: what if everyone rejects me, hates me, or casts me out? I am surely the only gay person on Earth. No one else feels like this. If I glance too long at that adorable guy, everyone will see and hate me. Paranoia takes root and you try even harder to get the gay to go away.

Then, one day, it's all just too much. No matter how scary it may be or how terrible the nebulous future may be it *has* to be better than living this lie. Fuck. This.

Knowing that somewhere there are others like you, you trust Fate and declare: "I am gay." Immediately balloons and glitter fall from the ceiling, a disco ball descends, and hugely loud and fabulous disco music blares. Two larger-than-life drag queens burst in covered with sequins and feathers, hand you a copy of *Ruling with a Sequined Fist*, pack a bag for you, and escort you off to the wonderland you always hoped existed on the other side.

Well, maybe not that last bit—but it will metaphorically happen after you learn how to be gay. You might think just *being* gay is enough, but it's not. You almost certainly had no gay role models growing up and as a result haven't learned the vocabulary, movements, eyebrow motions, and posturing of gay society. There is much work to be done, but you will be so fabulous afterwards!

Coming Out Is a Process

Coming out isn't something that happens once. Rather, it is a continual process—whenever you enter a new situation and feel safe enough you come out all over again. Maybe you already came out to your friends and family. Even so, every time you meet a new person or start a new job you come out all over again. This is okay. The main coming out process involves three steps:

Come out to yourself.
Come out to your friends.
Come out to your family.

If you're even considering coming out, you've probably wrestled with the notion and are close to identifying as yourself as a homosexual. Don't stress the labels too much yet—there's plenty of time for that later. There are many ways to come out and be gay and only one way to mess it up: ignoring your impulse to come out, getting married, having children, and otherwise burying yourself in hetero-normativity. Let's get started with you.

Terrible Coming Out Strategies
1) Walk in to your local truck stop restroom and shout "I'm gay" to the first person that stands next to you at the urinal.
2) Paint your face with rainbows and go to church Sunday morning.
3) Tell the cute boy working the grocery store checkout line while he's scanning your unusually large pile of cucumbers, bananas, and carrots.

Coming Out to Yourself

Staring out into the unknown not knowing what being gay means is challenging. I certainly won't be the first to say this, but it bears repeating: it will get easier. It's like joining any new group: there are cultural norms, signs, and signifiers that begin utterly foreign and end up thoroughly integrated into your personality. After being gay for some time you will be able to spot other gays on the street and have a life that might be completely unrecognizable to your old life. Then again, it might be nearly identical, but with added man-love. You will learn to be so fucking fabulous, you really will. But first you have to come out to yourself. You have to look inside and tell yourself "I am gay. It's awesome that I'm gay. A world more colorful and wonderful than the closeted one I currently inhabit is waiting on the other side." Just do it. It's okay if it's too scary to tell others at this point—just make sure to say it out loud even if you're alone.

There are loads of books and Websites giving coming out advice and a lot of it is good. A list is provided in Appendix A. If you are suicidal or feel you are in imminent danger then stop reading this page right now and go to those references. Come back here when you're ready to show the world how glorious you are. After allowing yourself to imagine the gay you, figure out whom to tell first. This will probably be a friend of yours.

Coming Out to Your Friends

It is quite possible your friends already know you are gay. You may be convinced you are passing as straight, but in reality you seem gayer than you realize. There are many, many subtle cues inherent to gay life you're probably affecting nearly by accident. Especially as you draw closer to coming out, these little things keep sneaking past your I'm-not-gay front. For example, straight men make eye contact far less frequently than gay guys. Straight guys tend not to swoon around hot guys. Oh yes, you're doing that—when your eyes get a little wider and you pay rapt attention to every word falling off your crush's lips. Yeah, straight guys swoon around girls, not each other. In short: your friends already suspect you're gay so just *come out already*.

You may be truly terrified these buddies will reject you, but you're probably mistaken. Some of your friends will not only be fine, but be thrilled for you and will join you at the gay bars. Others may not be so understanding. Some of your friends may be dropping subtle and not-so-subtle hints indicating they already know you're gay. Pay attention to these clues. Most importantly: don't pick your battles, pick your alliances. If your friends already suspect you're gay, then it really isn't a world-shattering realization to discover the truth everyone already knows. Your friends will most likely get a little weird for a while—the declaration is still as big to them as it is to you—but they will come around. If, for whatever reason, some of them don't: forget them. They weren't very good friends if they don't love you for who you are. There are so many people in this world that it isn't worth losing your mind over whether people will like the real you or not. It's better to be a beloved "true" you than a false-loved "false" you.

Coming Out to Your Family

Once you have a solidly on-board friend who is comfortable with gay-you it's time to consider whether it is wise to tell your family. This phase is especially tricky and it really helps to have sympathetic friends. If you live with your parents and have a sense you will be thrown out or suspect one of your family members may go ballistic and possibly harm you, you should stay incognito for now. If this is the case, focus on gaining support from your buddies and planning the steps required to get into a stable situation in order to come out to your family. Tell your family you are gay only once you feel safe. If you have to move out, so be it. If you're on your own two feet their power to hurt you is greatly diminished.

Research on coming out shows disclosure tends to go in this order: sister, mom, brother, and then dad last. According to the latest social science research, your family will have one of four possible reactions: loving denial, resentful denial, loving open, and hostile recognition. Don't fret if your family does not immediately accept your homosexuality. You wrestled with the notion, possibly for years, before telling them, so give them some space to process the information. Even if your parents suspect you're a bit light in the loafers, they still might not be 100% ready when you come out. It's a big deal and it takes time. Here are the four reactions explained a bit more:

Loving Denial (warm, deny)

Tag line: "You're my child and I love you, but don't talk to me about your boyfriend."

Loving denial is when your parents express that they care about you, but they will not accept your LGBT identity. Your well-meaning mother might keep asking if you met any nice girls lately, for example. Although this is better than being thrown out of the house, I would be most displeased that I would have to keep my fabulousity in check.

Resentful Denial (hostile, deny)

Tag line: "We will never speak of this again."

They reject your gay identity and are hostile about it. This happens when your parents get upset you told them and then attempt to destroy your LGBT identity. They might throw away found porn, try and "man" you up, or otherwise try and remove your queerness.

Loving Open (warm, acknowledge)

Tag line: "We love you. When are you bringing over the nice guy you've been talking about?"

This is what every guy dreams of when he comes out to his family. Your family accepts you are gay, acknowledges it, and wants you to be included in the family as you are. Don't over-celebrate this reaction if it's the first one, though, as fluctuation between reactions is common. Unfortunately, this is one of the less frequent initial responses, but is often what happens eventually.

Hostile Recognition (hostile, acknowledge)

Tag line: "There won't be no faggots living in my house. Get out!"

In this scenario, your family reacts by totally accepting you are LGBT and then removing you—and your queerness—from the situation. They recognize the gay identity and pick fights over it. They will attempt to belittle you for being gay.

Remember: it is very common that more than one of these reactions will happen over time. People react differently in a state of shock than they do after having some time to process. The change may be gradual. Please be patient and don't assume one day's feelings are a permanent opinion. Just because your folks act like horrible monsters now doesn't mean they will always feel this way. Don't fret—this part is difficult. If you're truly terrified you will get a hostile-recognition reaction, move out of the house or at least have a safe landing space set up in case things go poorly. Be brave; don't be stupid.

Before I move on, I realize some of you had a horrific coming out, your parents are abysmal, and you may have been outed by your friends or put in any number of compromising situations.

Because gay youth are prone to suicide attempts I'll say this to you: hang in there, Mary. I promise a big lavender world awaits you. Make it your goal to stick it out. For help with this, check out Kate Bornstein's book *Hello Cruel World*. Kate is the mother I will never be.

Meeting Your First Gays

Now that you're out it's time to make some gay friends! Thanks to the Internet there are tons of ways to do this along with more traditional routes. Although you *can* survive hanging out with just your straight buddies, you won't truly be on your way to being fabulous without a posse of gay friends and associates. At the very least, you need to gather a dating pool from somewhere. This is the beginning of your journey from being the recently out guy you are now to glamour personified. We all start somewhere.

> **Gay Terms of Endearment—Retro and Modern**
> Mary
> Nancy
> Dorothy
> Sister
> Honey
> Bitch

The first place to look for other gays is the gay bar. Traditionally, this was a major place in gay society. Gays would meet in the super-safe space of the gay bar to make friends, see their first drag queen, find potential dates, and find overnight companions. Although attendance has been steadily declining in most gay bars since online hookup Websites stole most of the looking-for-sex gay men, it actually reframed many bars in a positive way. You'll still be cruised, but now gay bar attendees tend to go increasingly for community and camaraderie. The first trip to the gay bar is still a right of passage for new gays, so you should check it out sooner rather than later. It will be much more fun and much less scary than you anticipate.

Throughout the rest of this book you will learn myriad other ways to meet, befriend, and peacock for and around other homos. You will learn of gay neighborhoods and vacation towns; gay jobs; gay events; gay sports leagues; gay fighting; and all about the massive, global queer community breathlessly awaiting your arrival.

So now you've come out, begin shaking off the vestiges of the limiting closet-case you used to be, and met some gay people. In order to fully join gay society you must learn the four gay society survival skills: glamour, filth, camp, and divinity. With polish, these four skills will take you very far in queer society and make you the queen/king you know you are.

Queer Social Domains (The Four Gay Humours)

Establishing Dominance

We will now build the foundation of your delicious gay life. I will teach you the secrets of the sequined fist. These are the four critical gay social skills—the nuts and bolts of gayness. The better you've developed them the more sequined your fist will be. They are called the four gay humours.

In ancient times, people believed the human body was composed of four elements: blood, phlegm, yellow bile, and black bile representing the four elements of air, water, fire, and earth, respectively. When your four humours were in balance, the thinking went, you were healthy. Imbalances produced both physical illnesses and *personality* changes. Fast forward to today: aside from some very strange kinksters, we no longer believe in the four humours, but the notion of elements in balance, a skill ecosystem, has risen to replace it. By coming out and joining the ranks of the gay mafia you get the four keys to the queer kingdom: glamour, filth, camp, and divinity. These are the four skills gays cultivate and excel at as a group. These are the four gay humours. We're going to unpack these in a little bit.

By tapping into all four of these skills and mixing them as deftly as possible, you will earn a PhD in faggotry. Naturally, these skills have varying levels of effectiveness for each person and use should be kept in moderation with balance between the four. Having one skill overdeveloped to the detriment of others causes imbalance. Using filth without glamour makes you creepy. Being divine without camp makes you an asshole. Worst of all, continuous reliance on the four gay humours builds immovable emotional walls—too much and you're a sociopath—all artifice, no personality. These are all social tools, a way of producing a fabulous set of masks, skills, habits, and self-knowledge for socializing—they are certainly not meant for 24/7/365 use. In the other direction, having a complete lack of each will make you the most unappetizing meathead imaginable. Strive for something in between.

Glamour is the ability to amplify and diminish traits to publicly present the desired image of you. **Filth** is the removal of shame revolving around sexual practices both conventional and esoteric. One only embraces this trait when the word filth is a compliment rather than an insult. This is especially important in America where there is an ingrained sense of shame about sexuality. **Camp** is the exaggeration of the serious and conventional to the point of absurdity and realizing social norms are rules meant to be broken. It is also taking delight in the absurd theatricality of everyday life. Finally, **divinity** is not divine in the deity-sense, but rather the "I am *divine*" sense. It is cultivating the confident part of yourself to excel in all you pursue. All gay people have these four traits in varying degrees and should attempt to cultivate each. I see guys who live lives where some of these skills are radically underdeveloped. A life without them is grey and dreary.

In case this all still seems terribly murky to you, I've devised a scale with our queer skills in place so you see where you might stack up. After finding your place on the four spectrums, each facet will be covered in greater detail. One means you lack the skill. Two means you have it, but just barely. Three means you have an average amount. Four

> Four Humour Scoring Sheet:
>
> **1** No Skill
> **2** Present, But Marginal
> **3** Average
> **4** Fully Cultivated
> **5** Too Far. All Artifice.

means you've fully cultivated it. Five means you've gone way, way overboard. In other words, an average of one is hopeless, and a five insane and borderline inhuman. Ready? Ok, let's put on the sorting wig and see where you lie:

The Faces of Glamour

Skill in glamour is defined by your ability to successfully project the persona you want others to see.

Glamour 1: You know that dream where you're in front of an audience and you suddenly realize you're naked. A score of glamour one means your entire life is like that. You lack the ability to amplify what you want others to see and diminish what you would rather keep private. When in public you are ill suited for the occasion. We all have things we want others to notice and skeletons meant to stay hidden in our closets and with no skill in glamour you cannot manage the information surrounding yourself.

Glamour 2: When you have a trait you think is cool or valuable, you hide it. You are socially awkward and present a less than enviable front. You may have plenty of wonderful things to share with the world, but you cannot make the world listen. Anxiety prevails when all eyes fall on you. When you make an attempt to put up a public façade you "choke" and everyone sees right through it.

Glamour 3: All of your clothes fit properly. You know how to spin most facts to make yourself look better. You can get along with some different types of people, but complex social interactions make you look silly. You can switch gears between interacting with different associates with little difficulty, but get flustered when calibrating your presented personality to new types of people.

Glamour 4: Everything you own looks great on you. You feel great in all your clothes—your style matches who you are. Everything you do involving public performance—be it theater, singing, storytelling, speaking—seems effortless and filled with stage presence. You look perfectly comfortable everywhere you go. You know your flaws, you know your strengths, and know the face you want to present to the world. You know how to divulge your flaws when you choose. Although you crafted a well-developed public persona, you can drop it and become real you when the situation requires it. You are hardly ever caught with the wrong face on.

Glamour 5: You are a trend. Everyone who meets you wants to be your groupie. They grovel at your feet for mere acknowledgement of their presence. Your parties are legendary. Your public persona is so enormous in scope and invulnerability that at least one person wants to see you dead. You are wholly immodest. You can face hostility and compliments with equal grace, because you are utterly fearless. You know you are truly the wittiest, best dressed, and most interesting person you have ever met. This is the only part of you anyone ever sees. Your close associates get slowly unnerved that you are no longer a person and are, in fact, a caricature. Chances are you have no real friends. You're all frosting, no cake. You are too much. You are so adept at showing people what you want them to see that people fail to see the rest of you.

The Faces of Filth

Skill in filth requires a lack of shame regarding your sexual needs and desires as well as those of your partners.

Filth 1: Because you experience sex as shame, your sexual repertoire is limited. When you have a sexual encounter with someone you feel disgusted afterwards. You may even feel shameful and disgusting *while* you are having sex. You feel immense guilt and negative feelings surrounding your desire for sex. You think sex is limited to penetration and masturbation. The mere idea of discussing sex makes you uncomfortable, and not aroused-uncomfortable.

Filth 2: You realize sex can be fun. You try out sexual activities and they might feel good at the time, but you feel bad afterwards. You may have had a few hookups. Although you do not generally feel shameful when having sex, the feelings come up soon after you finish. You may purposefully engage in sex acts you perceive as especially shameful. All shame-based fetishes grow here. You do not discuss your sexual appetites and inclinations and feel uncomfortable when others discuss theirs.

Filth 3: A willingness to experiment with and discuss sexual proclivities you feel comfortable about defines an accomplished level-three filth maven. You don't sexually stray past where you feel extremely comfortable. Sometimes you feel deeper urges, but you don't generally explore them. You probably have some hidden fantasies you're scared to share. You don't judge anyone for their sane and consensual sexual behavior. You know what you want and try some new things, but still get uncomfortable if your partner expresses a desire you're unfamiliar with.

Filth 4: You are sexually confident and entirely shame-free. You truly know sex can be a total adventure. You are fine with a range of sexual practices and can fluidly indulge and experiment in both the conventional and unusual. Friends and associates come to you when they need sex advice. You help others become sexually actualized and follow their desires. Your partners never fear asking you to try something new. You never say ought or should in the context of sex.

Filth 5: You fetishize sex—you're so beyond the sense of shame that you embody sex for sex's sake. Sex is your master, not your servant. You have so little shame that you invoke shame in others. You express to your partner what makes you feel good and what gets you off, though your partners by this point may be interchangeable—it's about what gets you off. You are so comfortable with your sexuality that you share your desires and needs with nearly anyone who might listen, even if they're horrified, vaguely or otherwise. Your desire for exciting sex borders on obsession.

The Faces of Camp

Camp focuses on social rules. Discovering that all our social choices are simply conventions and can be broken is a hallmark of camp.

Camp 1: You take everything seriously. If something smells of classlessness you won't even look at it. You always do what is done. You do it so much and so completely that you are unaware of your choices. When others depart from accepted behaviors and interests you are horrified. Choosing media, food, and all cultural accoutrement comes naturally because you know exactly what you *should* choose. Sometimes people seem to think your devotion to the rules is funny, but you never understand why.

Camp 2: You mostly do what is done, but sometimes sneak out for a rule break. It is sometimes too onerous a task to always follow *all* the rules. Besides, willfully breaking them on rare occasions releases the pressure of having such enormous cultural norms to follow all the time. You have a vague sense that breaking social norms can feel good. What's more, it can be fun and funny.

Camp 3: You have a sense that taste is a series of choices. You begin to match your authentic choices accordingly. You feel a vague sense of freedom from the "oughts" and "shoulds" of this world, but they still come back when you divert too far from your set path. Maybe you've seen some exploitation films or giggled your way through *Mommie Dearest*.

Camp 4: By knowing taste is a series of choices, you can now exaggerate good choices to the point where they become bad ones. Conversely, bad choices can be so perfectly bad they become good. You have the ability to exaggerate and lampoon the arbitrariness of the rules. Whenever something is exaggerated it becomes glorious. You can readily identify and delight in failures of art, music, food, seriousness, or humanity. Additionally, the more someone takes something seriously—especially when it is unmerited—the funnier it seems. You may feel you do not seem to fit into a class or culture due to how authentically you follow your own desires.

Camp 5: Your failure to take things seriously is so extreme that things meant to be taken seriously are not. Your whole life is "irony" to the point where you see only the humor, not the humanity. People look like a collection of cultural choices to you rather than humans.

The Faces of Divinity

Skill in divinity produces self-confidence and the blossoming of art from within and the ability to successfully interact and converse with others.

Divinity 1: You lack confidence. When people—even strangers—demand things you immediately submit. You tend to be a people pleaser doing things that pleasure others and not you. "Door mat" is a good description of your personality. You lack cultural aspirations. You don't pursue wit, art, or things that emanate from within. Attempts at jokes sound like you're telling a tragic story. Your apartment looks like you just moved in, even though you've lived there for two years. You spend all your nights in front of the television. People find you boring.

Divinity 2: You strictly avoid any form of publicity. You shy away when people recognize you. You realize you have some skills, but would never dare assert yourself or display your skills in any way that might get you noticed or have a risk of failure. You may remain quiet nearly all the time, but once in a while you come out with a zinger. You have a secret appreciation for art or music. You prefer to remain invisible though your friends know there's more to you.

Divinity 3: When you feel safe you let out the brilliant, witty person inside. When you are in new situations or otherwise outside your safety zone you retreat. You sometimes get and appreciate compliments. You realize you have skills and talents and use them even though you sometimes pass credit on to others perceived as more deserving. You are gifted at teamwork, but never aspire to leadership. Your friends appreciate you and the things you do, but you never believe in yourself as much as they believe in you.

Divinity 4: You know what you're good at and are not shy at telling others this fact. You can perform, present, and be present in any situation knowing you are lovely and others might learn your loveliness. As opposed to glamour, where others perceive you as amazing, with divinity you feel amazing inside. You have seemingly effortless confidence and others notice your assertiveness. If someone gave you a microphone and told you to rock out (metaphorically speaking), you could. Everyone would applaud. You are divine.

Divinity 5: You spend your entire life in what amounts to a drag character even if you never put on makeup. You are so convinced of your own fabulousness that no one could ever tell you otherwise. You are immune to criticism. Even the most mundane slight is occasion to destroy someone socially. You are so singularly awesome that you are truly, utterly alone.

Are you finding yourself along these scales? If so, good for you! If not, no problem. In this section, I will describe what each humour is and is not and give you advice to help tone up or tone down your humours as required.

Glamour

Many people think glamour is an aura of alluring beauty, but they are mistaken. Attractive young gays may think they're inherently glamorous, but they're not. You see, pretty young things project an attractive front that is entirely interchangeable (it's the youth that's attractive, not their winning personality) and when you have glamour you're not just appealing, you're charismatic. Any old twink has abs that launch a thousand ships and would look hot dressed entirely in polyester, but glamour is something cultivated. If you've ever seen *The Craft*, you know the trashy 90's Goth girl glamour: an illusion making your hair look better or making you appear as a different person entirely. They bring us much closer to the concept. Glamour, in the queer sense, is the amplification of persona via the effortless execution of desired appearance and publicly performed skills. It is managing the information surrounding yourself—being your own PR agent. Glamour is the masquerade surrounding attention—amplifying a consciously chosen style and skill set so you look impossibly fabulous.

The first step in mastering glamour is identifying the attributes you've got. What do you want to put on parade? The second rule is identifying what you want to vague up. Everybody has these things—they can be related to your appearance, your personality, or even your emotional baggage. When you know what you want to showcase and conceal you're on your way. Let's look at an example of something you might want to hide.

For example, you're a bit overweight and want to snag someone a bit slimmer and fitter than you. What do you do? Sulk in the corner and call yourself a fatty? Become totally withdrawn and slam back shots of whisky until you can't see? Bake your feelings into a cake and eat the whole thing? No! You dress for your body type. Wear a knit shirt with thick seams that lay well along your shoulders. By calling attention to your shoulders, you pull it away from your belly. The same is true of hats, colored contacts, and outrageous hairstyles. "Pay no attention to that belly behind the curtain!" It is the attempt to make people look at something particular instead of, say, something they dislike, which is a first-level glamour.

Check yourself in the mirror right now. Do you have a nice butt? Of course you do. Knowing this, we must amplify it. People are not going to see that butt in baggy jeans. You need to wear something fitting that shows off your delightful derriere.

In order to succeed at glamorous presentation, employ the following strategy:

1) Identify people whose sense of style you really admire. They could be wearing anything from clever t-shirts to haute couture—anything appealing to you will work.

2) Go out and try to find similar items and wear them out.

3) See how people react. If you get compliments, keep it. Scrap it if you raise eyebrows—unless, of course, that's what you hope to achieve. Either way, be sure your new fashion is noticeable and attracts the people you seek.

4) After practicing a while with mimicry, try scouting out and gathering your own items.

5) Test each item, figure out what works in each context and how best to combine pieces, and you're on your way to being visually glamorous.

Now we're halfway there—we have the clothes and the body, now let's amplify or diminish aspects of your personality.

After getting the right look, you want to figure out how to put your best face forward: this is where personality-level glamour is required. In order to achieve this you'll need to first realize your projected personality is malleable and that, by treating your daily social encounters as a conscious experiment, you can achieve renown for your strongest talents. In order to succeed, try to think it through.

What are things about your personality you want to amplify? What's going on around? Are nearby people extroverted? What do they value? Should you be aggressive, hilarious, sheepish, awash in subcultural knowledge? For example, say you're at a bar where there's one group where the wit is flying. You jump right in and send out a bullet of your own. Near them, another group is talking about the psychological impact of the recession. The cute guy in the glasses seems particularly distressed. What do you do? You look at him and in a sobering voice say, "The American Dream is dead." Then, aloud, you share your well-informed thoughts on the matter. Follow this process to engage in finding the right face:

1) Figure out the values of the group you care to interact with. Is it cult film knowledge? Sports statistics? Perhaps everyone is discussing the new musical on Broadway.

2)   After figuring out what knowledge set they expect you to have, determine how they speak. Is everyone pleasant and supportive? Vicious and catty? Full of obscure quotes and erudite phrases?

3)   What do they expect of you? Do people describe you as "the living end?" Are you meant to be a silent observer? What about posture? Should you be slouchy and gruff or upright and uptight? This step will change over time since groups will expect different things at different times.

4)   Combine what this group values, how they present themselves, and what is expected of you into a single façade. Present this face to them.

5)   Repeat this process each time you interact with this group as well as others.

After a number of successes your confidence will increase and you will be able to effortlessly display these fronts. The easier it seems for you to put forth enviable fronts, the more glamorous it is. Make sure not to mention that you practiced endlessly in your bedroom and studied subcultural niches for weeks. Your ultimate goal is to get so fantastically talented at presenting such a flawless impression of yourself you don't seem to be trying at all. The emphasis here is, of course, on public performance.

Remember: clothing is your first line of defense in the world. People make myriad assumptions based on what someone wears. Think about how you react when seeing people in faded flannel and jeans versus a tailored suit. There are endless, complex, class and taste choices behind a single outfit and people react in surprising ways to changes in fashion. Your outfit alone can make you look approachable, intimidating, sexy, or whatever else you can pull a look together to project. Since fashion feedback tends to be immediate it is a great place to start, shallow though it may seem.

Let's say you want to be the queen of the club kids. First, obviously, you would have to find the club kids with the best fashions (style identification). Then you'll want to try and mimic a seen style (aping identified outfits). Figure out what does and doesn't get a reaction (fashion testing). Next, try and add your own flair (moving past mimicry). After enough successes you'll get a sense of what colors, fabrics, makeup styles, heel heights, and accessories combine to make you most notable and you can develop your own style (self-styling).

At the same time, aside from fashion, you'll have to perfect a whole range of performance skills so as not to be a very beautiful mannequin. First, you need to identify the status-gaining values required (identification of knowledge and values). In this case, some examples are: impeccable and witty conversation skills almost entirely wrapped in pleasantries and gossip, the ability to wear strange footwear and/or headpieces, a good walk, the ability to either throw or attend fabulous parties, and a good look for photos. Next, figure out how they perform in their group (identification of performing style). Does swishing increase as the day goes on? When taking a photo, what kind of face does everyone make—sneering, smiling, fashionable poses? Next, figure out what your role is. You may be the leader of the group or a relative newcomer (identification of your role). If you want to rule the world, you should of course try and make your role nominally more important with each interaction. Or, if you're a bloodthirsty type, just go for the jugular and the coup. Repeat this process for each club kid clique and voila—you are glamorous.

Now consider the reverse of the amping-up process. Remember back to when you were in the closet. You employed your glamour skills, but in reverse. You purposefully dressed and monkey-walked with your knuckles as near the ground as possible to look like a straight. Maybe you had a "girlfriend" who you were publicly dating, but in reality she was your devoted fag hag. Even though the presented front was false it was probably artfully designed. You dressed like a straight, walked and talked like a straight, and attempted to project a straightsville-persona. Thankfully, those days are over, but keep in mind how exhausting it is to keep up a false front. If you push glamour too far your looks may break and you'll suddenly find yourself quoting Derrida to vapid queens and other unsightly front-mismatches. Trust me, it's not a good look. Use glamour wisely.

Filth

Filth is developing a complete lack of sexual shame and a sex-positive attitude. Filth should come from a special place in your heart, the heart behind your scrotum. The heart that, when you look at your beautiful boyfriend, makes you want to slap his face with your dick. American culture breeds sexual shame and only the deviant overcomes it. Some misguided breeders consider being gay to be deviant all by itself. So they meet a "nice" girl, get married, have kids, become a company man, and sneak off to the adult bookstore to suck dick. Uh-oh! Someone couldn't deal with his filthy side. Being gay used to convey an automatic filth badge for performing illegal-at-the-time activities like cock sucking and anal sex. However, now that it's fashionable for girlfriends to take a shot in the mouth that's no longer the case—filth had to be redeveloped.

To be sexually fulfilled sex has to stop being scary. It's fun. You don't have to be married to have sex. You don't even need to know the guy's name. There are infinite ways to have sex and someone, somewhere, wants to try them with you. Forget everything you've been taught by conventional, terrified-of-sex society and start exploring your desires. The sooner you start trying different kinds of sexual events the sooner the fun ones become apparent.

Filth does not mean kinky although it can. Vanilla does not mean lack of filth although it can. Filth is identifying what brings you pleasure and expressing it without shame. What you identify can be as vanilla as cuddles and as kinky as fisting. Ignore the little voice saying to be ashamed of sex—listen to the one that gets your dick hard.

Tom of Finland, famous queer artist, followed the great internal trajectory of developing his own filth. As a young Finnish faggot he had access to large quantities of one of the all-time greatest gay male jerk-off fantasies: lumberjacks. While a young man, he started drawing pictures of the lumberjacks all around him. They were lithe, hairless, and looked like teenagers pretending to be lumberjacks because Tom of Finland was also projecting his sexuality onto them. Over time these pubescent images of masculinity turned a dark corner. They grew mustaches and bulging muscles. Their cocks became grotesquely exaggerated. They wore many tropes of manliness—police uniforms, construction worker gear, biker gear, etc. He followed his less conventional sexual desires along their full path—he didn't stop and say, "OMG, giant nipples are just too weird. I should draw flowers instead." No, he felt the urges inside him, accepted them, and then drew them. Just like that.

Until you've wandered into your own dark corners, you have no idea who you are. Staying in the family-values appropriate light only lets the chasm of desire grow until it comes out in strange ways—like a priest who "accidently" dies with a rope tied around his neck, a gas mask on, and his pants pulled down. Deal with your sexuality and all its pleasures and it has a much lower chance of killing you. The key is getting over the strange, conditioned American urge to recoil at the thought that sex can be fun, can involve all sorts of fluids and objects, and should be shared and discussed rather than hidden.

You may be thinking, "Oh, well, I'm so vanilla that this doesn't apply to me." You, my dear, are mistaken. You may not desire unusual things, but you can still take the time to discover what your real inclinations are. For example: do you like sucking dick, getting your dick sucked, or mutual oral? They are three different activities with different inclinations. At the end of the day, you are responsible for your own orgasm and the sooner you figure out what *really* gets you off and get over

> What are you into? Try listing a few things:
> 1)
> 2)
> 3)
> 4)
> 5)

any possible, associated moral dilemmas, the faster you'll be on the path to better sex. Here's a good fantasy test: turn off the porn and jerk off using only your imagination. Fantasize about things you've thought about trying in bed and see how turned on you get. If you get off in your head (and it's safe, consensual, and realistically possible), then by all means try it. Trying things does not mean doing them every day forever. If you require another exercise, remember that the gay vernacular implies filth with the question "what are you into?" The true filth maven should be able to answer that question unabashedly. So, what are you into?

Fortunately, gay men often develop a good idea of what they like to do in bed and any behavior you have happens more commonly than you think—the chances that you have a singular sexual urge are vanishingly small. Additionally, gay society permits sexual discussion far more than the straights do, so ask around for new things to try if you've got the desire. The sooner you stop feeling bad about your sexuality, go out, and fuck the way you want, the happier you'll be. Being gay puts you in a good position to get your rocks off in myriad ways—so go do it already!

Camp

The experiences of camp are based on the great discovery that the sensibility of high culture has no monopoly upon refinement. Camp asserts that good taste is not simply good taste; that there exists, indeed, a good taste of bad taste...The discovery of the good taste of bad taste can be very liberating. The man who insists on high and serious pleasures is depriving himself of pleasure; he continually restricts what he can enjoy; in the constant exercise of his good taste he will eventually price himself out of the market, so to speak. Here camp taste supervenes upon good taste as a daring and witty hedonism. It makes the man of good taste cheerful, where before he ran the risk of being chronically frustrated. It is good for the digestion.

--Susan Sontag, "Notes on 'Camp'"

One should either be a work of art, or wear a work of art.

--Oscar Wilde

You know that guy who drinks expensive wines, eats cheese imported from obscure towns in Eastern Europe, and sneers dramatically at the mere *idea* that some people eat macaroni and cheese? He's not very campy. However, consider the guy who sees a terrible movie and then calls you and says, "You just have to see [the movie]. It was delicious." Oh yeah, he's your man. You see, the first person follows all the "rules" of good taste while the other can identify things that violate social rules in a naïve and hilarious way. Camp is the process of refining and proclaiming good taste in terrible things—and doing it well. Camp is a branch of informatics using kitsch for data. Porn, particularly bad porn, is camp. The Las Vegas Strip is camp. Camp is a bite-sized irony snack. Indeed, there is skill in knowing the brilliance of trashiness and forced class and how radical unpretentiousness can be *hilarious*. There is skill in identifying and enjoying art that aimed very high and failed exquisitely. Not just failed, of course, but hit the precise, perfect failure in relation to its ambitions so the effort practically juxtaposed itself. Humor is the key here. To be campy one must laugh at seriousness, laugh at people who laugh at you, and fully enjoy life's madness.

Camp is also a way of life. You can easily liberate yourself from the pursuit of high pleasures and conventional, exclusionary snobbery by willingly turning back at the gates of high culture. If you begin to truly look around you—at what everyone is doing, saying, eating, drinking, and judging all who briefly misstep in the quest for taste, you begin to see how completely arbitrary and bizarre the conceptions of high taste are. If you need some help conceptualizing camp, try this exercise: whenever you're recommending something—art, movies, restaurants, etc.—insert the item into the following phrase spoken in a heavy New Jersey accent: "Go see [insert thing]. It's real classy." Try it out loud on a few dozen things—feel free to use a regionally appropriate accent—and you will find that, when uttered, the inserted nouns fall into three camps:

1) The ironic distance is too far: "Go read some Baudelaire. He's real classy."

2) The ironic distance is too close: "Put on this gold chain. It's real classy."

3) The ironic distance is just right: "Go see Twilight. It's real classy."

Since this is forced camp—and camp works best when naïve—try to imagine someone speaking the sentences in a very genuine way. Another good practice is the "quote" exercise. Pick a noun, put it in quotes, and list some examples. What is the difference between a movie and a "movie"? Testing ironic distance is a wonderful way to map your local camp contours—things perceived as campy vary wildly between social classes, professions, identities, and geographic regions.

Although dancing in the taste hinterlands is a great time, remember that *authenticity* should well up in the wake of camp. After discovering the theatricality of life it's a short leap to realizing that, since the blind leading the blind draws these cultural borders, you should make choices based on what you really like without overstressing the consequences. Sure, it's wonderful to show off your impeccable taste in both the sublime and the excessive, but remember that this daring hedonism should ultimately improve your life. Make fewer rules and more camp.

Once you have a sense of when things are campy, it's time to *exaggerate*. Since you know what a good ironic distance looks like, try and push it to the extreme. Don't settle for funny, reach for *the funniest thing in the entire universe*. Don't settle for a little glitter when you can have so much glitter that when you sneeze, glitter rains out from your nose. Expanding the scale of the borders and ludicrously overdoing it are the final points of camp. What does extremity look like? Watch *Mommie Dearest* or *Black Swan* and find out. The characters in those movies don't have anything approaching common emotions or experiences. Everything for them is magnified well beyond human levels. In extremity there is humor. That's why drag queens have such high eyebrows.

While struggling to learn camp, remember that Susan Sontag astutely attributed camp sensibility to gay people: "The peculiar relation between camp taste and homosexuality has to be explained. While it's not true that camp taste is homosexual taste, there is no doubt a peculiar affinity and overlap...so, not all homosexuals have camp taste. But homosexuals, by and large, constitute the vanguard—and the most articulate audience—of camp." She gave the gays the critical charge to uphold camp and all it stands for. She goes on to argue that gay men pin societal acceptance on aesthetic prowess and camp is, without a doubt, the most festive way to engage in this time-honored practice. These claims do require some further questioning—why would gays use camp as an aesthetic tool?

Outsider status breeds camp sensibilities. Gays, no matter how accepted we become, still exist outside the dominant straight paradigms, and are thus outsiders. Large facets of the straight life narrative are mostly useless to gays. One way to demonstrate the outsider feelings known to breed camp is to go hang out with all the straight people you used to be friends with before coming out. After venturing back from fairyland into straightsville, everything that straight people do seems foreign. The whole hetero universe should, by this point in your queer development, seem full of rituals and handshakes taken with the utmost seriousness. You can't throw a ping-pong ball into a cup and you're how old? Your handshake doesn't break at least three bones? You dance? Clearly, you cannot do the straight guy series of dick-size assessing activities. By not only failing at this, but discovering that it's quite silly, you have great leverage, the great leverage of the outsider. Now you can develop a sense not bound by breeder hang-ups like continuous tests of manliness—indeed, things perfectly abhorrent to straights can be your playground.

Playing in this territory is tricky, though, because the trap of being taken seriously about campy things always looms. If people think you would *actually* and authentically like to be seen wearing leopard-print pants you are in grave danger. Think back to the Jersey accent test and how it would feel if things you ironically attempted were in the "ironic distance too short" category. However, talking about terrible things as though they are *the funniest thing you have ever seen in your entire life* can make even the most detestable of interests quite acceptable. It helps if the people who would normally do this thing would treat it as near sacrosanct.

Along with simply juggling piles of kitschy things, camp teaches the great art of playing with expectations and pointing out the gross exaggerations taking place in everyday life. It is a form of comedy based on being fully aware of routine social nuances. What makes camp funny is not simply that people are doing something dreadfully tacky; it is realizing the perfection of its failure or its extreme excess. Consider video games. Michael Clarkson, blogger behind Discount Thoughts, puts it this way: "A certain camp spirit pervades almost all of gaming culture. Consumers seem to desire, and reviewers love to extol, games that embrace a certain degree of outrageous excess. Gamers love 'Over the top!' action, characters that live 'On the edge!,' art direction that's 'Out of this world!,' and storylines that are 'Epic!' Don't forget the exclamation marks, please. Video games rarely show any sense of restraint or refined sensibility; those that do rarely receive praise for it." So forget your sense of restraint and your refinement and camp it up.

Divinity

"I'm so beautiful. You gotta believe it I am beautiful. I'm so beautiful. Can't you see? Look at me!"

--"I'm So Beautiful" by Divine

"I don't care if you don't like my hair because I know it's amazing."

--"Amazing" by Hi-Fashion

Divinity is the supreme belief in your own fabulousness. It's the voice inside your head saying: "Is he looking at me? Why of course he is, darling—I am *amazing*." It's having a personal fanfare playing in your head whenever you enter a room. Some naysayers—never included among the divine—believe divinity ends with self-confidence alone. They simply do not understand the difference between conventional self-esteem and its cranked-up, glitter-snorting, alter ego divinity. Divinity, as it happens, scales along the masculinity spectrum—extremely butch men are generally not divine. They might be confident or well adjusted, but not divine. This is especially true when that "manliness" is an act. No—divinity is the armor that allows the femmy, the freaks, and the sideshow acts furthest from conformist queer living to walk outside, head held high.

When a young little gay boy sits in his room, fearful of the decidedly un-fabulous world outside, he begins to develop divinity. A teenage queer may have his face shoved in a toilet in reality, but in his mind he slowly becomes queen of his personal universe. Over time, he starts to develop a shield to protect him emotionally. Being gay, he dresses it up a little so his shield looks less like riot control shields and more like the shield of Achilles. Since we all need a way to process the rather unpleasant emotions of oppression, divinity is the conduit you push art through. When you feel like decorating your room, dying your hair, making a crazy dress made entirely from flip flops, painting, or engaging in any artistic pursuit you are practicing divinity. With enough practice two things happen:

1)   You get really good at your crafts and skills.

2)   You care less about what others think of them.

Hopefully these two aspects grow together. This is how art gets made and part of the reason gays have long produced many of the most incredible artists in history. We practice each and every day as a product of how the rest of the world feels about us. Straight society doesn't like you much? Make yourself *more awesome*.

When a young drag queen performs in a drag ball filled with talented queens, he struts his stuff and is essentially put on stage and ripped to pieces. Nobody looks good their first time in drag and the good-natured, but bad-mannered old queens are well aware of this and mercilessly try to undermine this young queen's look and confidence. This little drag queen, thoroughly humbled, goes home and cries—and then does it again. The next time nasty comments about the terrible makeup and lame outfit hurt less. It becomes increasingly less stressful to just be *out there* because, eventually, those nasty queens purposefully tearing her down taught her something—don't listen to those negative Nancy's. Eventually, this little queen turns into a fierce force to be reckoned with. The harder they push, the more she pushes back. Even if lots of hair and inches of heel are far from your mind, the sentiment remains. When you leave the house in the morning, you should feel like it's going to be a good day and you will own it, darling, because you are amazing.

Divinity works in tandem with glamour. Glamour is the public presentation of your fabulous self while divinity is the inner strength required to publicly present in the first place. Divinity is yin, glamour yang. They require each other, feed from one another, and both are necessary. Without glamour, self-confidence seems aggressive and unmerited. Without divinity, performances lack that *je ne sais quoi* required to take something from awesome to enviable. Together a gay man has the skills and the confidence to take on the world with glamour, his sword, and divinity, his shield.

Divine, the legendary drag queen, is a patron saint of divinity (it's not just a clever name). Here was a fat, odd-looking, radical gal who ate dog shit and mainlined eyeliner on film, and later became a disco star. Take that in for a moment. She wasn't beautiful. She wasn't sweet. She was purposefully disgusting and so motherfucking confident in that fact that she rose above the riffraff and into celebrity. She believed in herself and her art no matter what people said.

The truly divine are the dream chasers. They realize they have something to say and are not afraid to say it. Although artistic production requires failure, this humour builds the strength of character required to get up, brush yourself off, and try again. Eventually, output matches feelings and truly divine creations spring forth. Divinity is the fire making the steam driving the engine.

If you are not yet divine, you poor dear, then you better learn. There is, of course, a method to cultivating divinity. First, believe in yourself. Second, believe in yourself so damn much that you will stop at nothing to achieve your goals. A divine person is not afraid to make a joke. Or a movie. Or write a book. Or become a scientist. As you are believing in yourself, keep pursuing enriching things in life and continue sharing them with others. Figure out what makes you happy, and what you can do (and wear, for that matter) to proudly walk out of the house each day. When you try out a new fashion, make some obscene art, post a video online, or otherwise construct the physical manifestation of your internal fabulousness, just don't take no for an answer. The only way culture moves forward is when those with good ideas form thick enough skin to promote them. Be one of them. Be divine.

So now we've worked out the critical social skills—the foundation is laid, but who fills the house? It's time we toured the many, many kinds of gay people out there in the world. Some of them might be new to you and some old news, but after I introduce you around you'll hopefully be able to find your seat at the table.

The Gay Social Spectrum

As you've seen in the four humours, everyone has a place along the skill continuum, making us an interesting bunch of gays. In this section I will share the gays you will meet out and about. Remember that our community is diverse and there are many versions of us. This is not an exhaustive list and does not intentionally imply stereotypes. You can be one of the following gays and not behave exactly the way I describe it; you may identify with several or none of these descriptions, or may change with time or context. However, in order to recognize types of gays it helps to have a strong portrait.

There are an endless variety of gays. When you first enter gay society the sheer variety of vocabulary required to identify people is staggering. "You mean there are *kinds* of drag queens?" Yes. There are so many gay classes and subclasses of people they could fill a whole book, but the following set will give sufficient overview. It might seem impossible to parse who is which kind of gay and which gays sleep with one another, but the next page contains a handy map for identifying the vast majority of gay types and with whom they associate. Each line represents an alliance between two groups. Each line is assumed to be bi-directional. Groups, with the possible exception of closet cases, associate and ally with other members of their own tribe as well as those connected with lines. Stay at homos could come from any group and may casually associate with any group, but are not an active part of that group. Explanations of the types follow. Each gay group is listed below with its primary humours. Although certain members may have higher or lower scores, the primary humours most strongly identify members of the group.

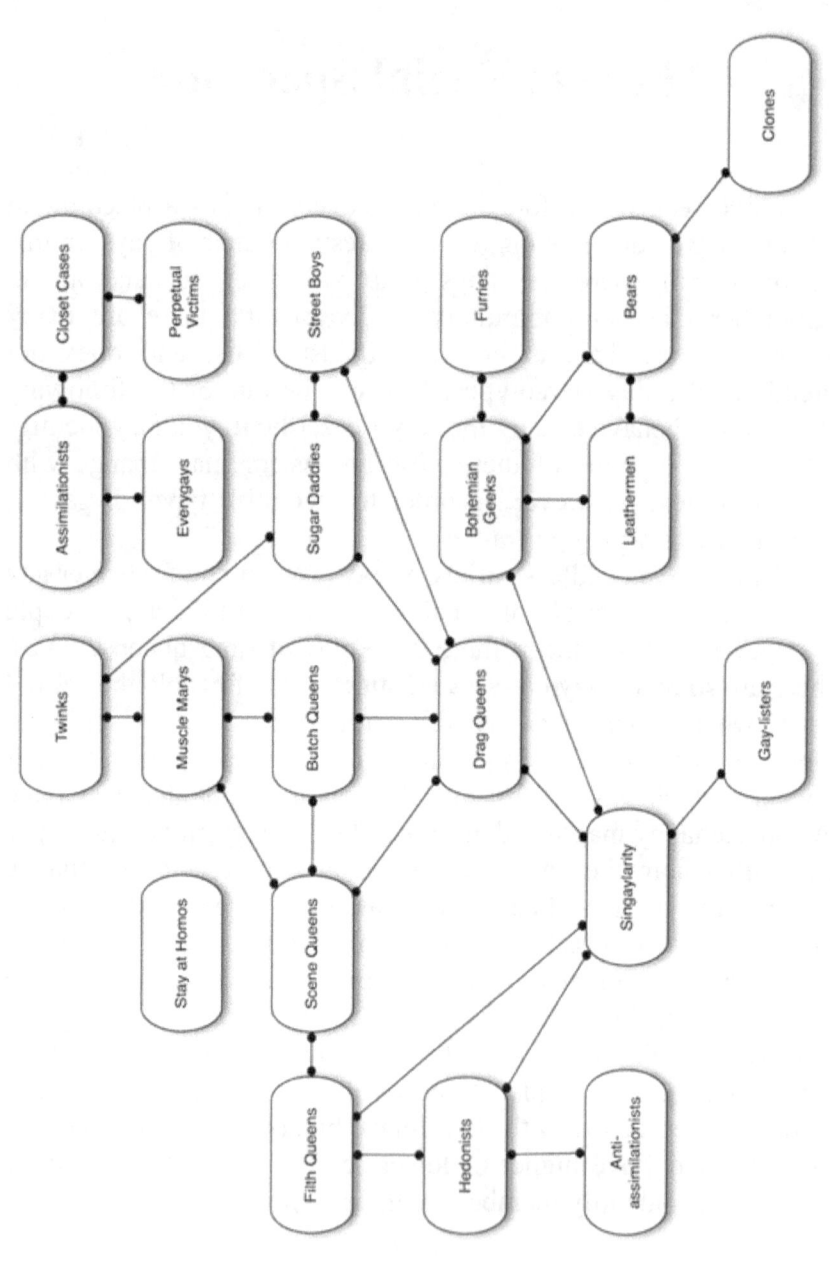

Hedonists

Primary Humours: filth, divinity

Hedonism is a life philosophy well suited to homosexuals. Hedonists are among the most dangerous company to keep if you don't know your limits. If you're, say, nineteen and your body can still take a lot of abuse—by all means find these people. The hedonistic lifestyle develops rapidly, but can become much more even-keeled over time, so it's best to start young as a fiery Hedonist and be able to survive into a more balanced sensualist. Hedonists, like all other fags, come in many forms. Let's first chat about what a hedonist is not. A hedonist is not someone wearing gaudy clothes and sunglasses at night smoking tina in the corner. That is a drug addict. A hedonist is not someone who goes to a hotel orgy every weekend where he gets gangbanged by thirty strangers. That's a well-oiled hole with a life-support system. A hedonist is a guy who lives life for pleasure—someone who sanely indulges himself until every outlet for delight has been tried.

They might have a martini every day. They have probably slept with all manner of people and are too, ahem, broad to have a "type." They might date three or four guys at a time and seem equally comfortable with all or none of them at one time. They drink the best drinks, eat the best food, go on the best vacations, throw the most outrageous parties, have the best sex, and are all around pleasure-seekers. If you find that dinner with friends, preceded and followed by cocktails, and ending with an adventure is your idea of the good life—you are probably a hedonist. If you ever quit a perfectly respectable job claiming it didn't make you happy enough and you're too busy following your dreams to care—you're a hedonist. If you are thoroughly confused by conventional bourgeois values you are probably a hedonist.

To take it a step further, this subset of gays pursues pleasure as a quest. It's not about bigger and better (except when it is), it's about following your inner desires to their end points and keeping everything that remains pleasurable. During the 1800s, hedonism morphed into the gay-famous philosophy called dandyism. Oscar Wilde, of course, is the most famous dandy/hedonist of all.

Hedonists are, however, sometimes mistaken as depressed, evil, dangerous, and a variety of other unsightly terms. If any of these things can be applied to someone you know who refers to himself as a hedonist, then they are not hedonists. Eating, drinking, or sexing your feelings is maladaptive. However, waking up and following your joy each day without a care in the world about how you're perceived—that's a true hedonist. Remember to follow the hedonist edict: "Everything in moderation. Including moderation."

Dates: other hedonists, filth queens, singaylaritys

Tricks: everything and anything

Avoids: assimilationists

Native habitat: the bedroom, the path of adventure

Drag Queens

"They live in the superficial
They don't know who I am
They want to take me for granted
But they don't know what I glam
I, I, I, am what I glam
Glam, glam, glam, glam I am."
--"I Am Glam" by Ze!
Primary Humours: glamour, camp, divinity

Drag queens are the VIPs of queer society. Since they are public figures in the local scene they are often seen out at local bars and clubs consistently attempting to raise money for charity and/or their own status. Ever fabulous, drag queens have been known to jump and inhabit styles ranging from nearly nude to high Victorian and everything in between. There are many types of queen and only a fool mistakes one type for another.

Glamzilla: Glam, GLAM, GLAMOUR!

This type of queen constructs an artifice of impenetrable and intimidating glamour. They create high fashion monster couture and revel in their own fabulousness. They wear at least two wigs (if not more) and turn drag into a high art. They sometimes sport costumes so impractical they can hardly move about with features like four-foot headdresses. When speaking to *glamzilla* queens it is expected that you will cower in their presence, as their taste is light years beyond your own. It is also expected that those lucky enough to speak to them construct entire conversations out of hyperbolic compliments. Anything less will get you the kind of tongue lashing you wouldn't want.

Trash Queens: CAMP Filth CAMP!

Trash queens subvert the idea of feminine glamour altogether and purposefully look terrible—nay, frightening—and are the closest thing to Tim Curry's character in *It* walking the streets. Generally, trash queens defend their indefensible style as being a reaction to a certain sector of drag culture's desire to "pass" or even to be "pretty." They use their jarring appearance and carefully crafted terror to keep their adoring—if slightly uncomfortable—audience shocked at their antics.

Genderfuck Queens: Camp, Divinity

Genderfuck queens cross masculine and feminine attire to question the notion of gender as a concept. The stereotypical outfit worn by these queens—nearly all of them do some variation at least once—is a tutu and combat boots. Combining hypermasculine and hyperfeminine signifiers, aside from getting all nearby semiologists hard, lets both the queen and the audience know that drag can be used as a tool to question notions of masculinity as well as femininity.

Performance Art: Divinity, Glamour, Divinity

Sometimes drag can be employed as a form of performance art. Naturally, in many ways, drag is *always* performance art. However, it is certainly possible to push the boundaries far enough to become more "art" and less "drag."

Female Impersonators: Camp, Camp, Glamour

Female impersonation, the old standby of drag, consists of dressing up as and behaving like a famous female. This style is old as the day is long and, as a result, occasionally goes dormant until a female worth emulating comes along. Some of the many women fit for impersonation are: Judy Garland, Bette Midler, Barbara Streisand, Tina Turner, Cher, Madonna, and Lady Gaga.

Dates: other drag queens, scene queens, butch queens, sugar daddies

Tricks: whomever they want—are you going to stop them?

Avoids: assimilationists

Native habitat: clubs, bars, balls, drag shows, fundraisers

Assimilationists

Primary Humours: glamour

Assimilationists are gay men obsessed with being accepted by straight society. In a world conditioned to believe that all gay men are borderline-socialist shopaholics, these guys emphatically break the mold. These are the people who chastise the bathhouse betties of the world and lead shockingly conventional lives. They aren't trying to "prove" anything with their way of life; it's just what comes naturally to them. They insist gays are exactly like everyone else and that gays should spend less time prancing about in glitter and daisy dukes and more time being well behaved, normal men. Historically, these men founded the homophile movement popularized by The Mattachine Society with their lesbian counterparts starting the Daughters of Bilitus. These are the people, love them or hate them, who fight for LGBT rights within polite society.

Dates: assimilationists, everygays, closet cases

Tricks: trade, closet cases, everygays, perpetual victims, gaylisters

Avoids: hedonists, singaylaritys, bohemian geeks, drag queens

Native habitat: The banal everday-everywhere; anything normal

Anti-assimilationists

"...The master's tools will never dismantle the master's house."

--Audre Lorde

Primary Humours: camp, filth

    Assimilationism's arch-nemesis, the anti-assimilationists, fight against racism and classism in the gay community and believe that promoting unconventional (i.e. non-heterosexual) ways of living will bring gay society forward, and perhaps lead the way to a saner humanity. These gays start a multitude of social, political, and charity groups providing community support without suggesting that we should attempt to look, act, or behave like straight people. Instead of promoting gay marriage, for example, an anti-assimilationist believes the government should be entirely removed from the marriage business and that no legal benefit should be gained from hyper-conventional monogamous coupling. Indeed, over time, these avant guard faggots have come up with infinite exciting modes of living. These are the people, love them or hate them, who fight for our rights in the streets.

Dates: in a post-modern fashion

Tricks: everyone except assimilationists

Avoids: normal people

Native habitat: activist groups, the anarchist bookstore

Everygays

Primary Humours: camp, divinity, glamour, and filth, but at low to undetectable levels

The everygay is the completely average gay. These are the people targeted by "the gay agenda." They probably don't live in gay neighborhoods, but they visit them on vacations. They dress like comparable straight guys save for better haircuts and slightly better clothing. They lead their lives amongst similar friends and occasionally indulge in a night out at the gay clubs, but never veer towards becoming scene queens. Advertising in gay magazines targets them. They own little to no costume clothing. They are the conventional, non-threatening product created by the gays-are-just-like-you 1990s. They were exceedingly rare when homosexuality was outlawed and completely stigmatized. However, their numbers increase every day as gays become increasingly mainstream. They sometimes get uncomfortable when lumped into a large group with the "freaks" of gay society, although some of them secretly covet the lives of those more extreme and socially integrated in gay society. In a future where homosexuality is completely de-stigmatized, the everygays will go to the gay bar the way "Irish" Americans go to the Irish pub.

Dates: everygays, assimilationists

Tricks: they would never admit to it

Avoids: anti-assimilationists, scene queens, hedonists, singaylaritys

Native habitat: living their lives

The Singaylarity

"In an expanding universe, time is on the side of the outcast. Those who once inhabited the suburbs of human contempt find that without changing their address they eventually live in the metropolis."

--Quentin Crisp

Primary Humours: glamour, filth, camp, divinity-all fully developed (4+)

A singaylarity is someone who has mastered all four humours. They may be poets, playwrights, chefs, sex workers, or artists of any kind, and more likely than not they make their everyday lives into art. They are generally heavily associated with the arts because when you have a delicious wit, a devastating look, and lead a completely shame-free existence, everyone listens to you and tries to see what you see. A singaylarity lives much of his life in the near future because he paves out the present with the choices he makes in his everyday life. Months, years, or decades after a singaylarity loves something, the everygays devour it. He is the tastemaker.

Even a cursory glance through queer history produces a long list of these men. Oscar Wilde, Andy Warhol, Tennessee Williams, Tom Ford, and most other famous gays you can think of are so skilled in their humours that they rose to the top.

It's easy to spot a singaylarity: you can *feel* his presence when he enters a room. His personality seems to fill the whole place up, though he is but one man. The most important people in the vicinity will immediately greet him and the aura surrounding him is one of perfection. His clothes will be perfect for the context. His conversations will be perfect. His skills will be in demand. His refined and camp tastes are perfect. He is perfection.

A singaylarity is not a hipster. Hipsters care *only* about artifice and not about the substance behind it. They work the trends, but never actually start them. They are a demographic, while the singaylaritys are the sparks causing the fire. As an historical example, remember there were only six *actual* beats: Allen Ginsberg (gay), William Burroughs (gay), Jack Kerouac (straight), Neal Cassidy (gay), Greg Corso (pretty straight), and Herbet Huncke (gay)—most everyone else was akin to what is now a hipster. See a pattern here?

Dates: singaylaritys, hedonists, drag queens, gaylisters, filth queens

Tricks: anything and everything

Avoids: assimilationists, scene queens, anything common

Native habitat: the dark

Bohemian Geeks

Primary Humours: divinity, camp

Bohemian geeks play strategy board games (*The Settlers of Catan, Ticket to Ride, etc.*), like geeky media for its camp value, read vast amounts of comic books and graphic novels mixed in with geek-friendly philosophers like Buckminster Fuller and Ray Kurzweil, and probably have at least one piece of eight-bit inspired art around their house. In addition to being good gamers and well read, they are really, really nerdy. They follow the ins and outs of internet and video game cultural and generate memes with such rapid speed the Internet can barely produce enough content to entertain them.

Geeky bears are a special subset of bohemian geeks. As geeks often have sedentary office employment and hobbies requiring lots of sitting, many become a bit rotund, grow beards, and take on the appearance of bears. However, this is not always the case. Geeks are the other notable subset of queers, aside from bears, who delight in beards and body hair.

Geeks follow a separate set of social codes than normal faggots. The main noticeable difference is that geeks accept hugely bizarre character eccentricities. Remember, while you might have been the popular party animal in high school that blew the football team in dark rooms, these kids hung out with the freaks. Hanging out with the freaks has its benefits and drawbacks, but one of the important differences is this: everyone, no matter how strange, is allowed to be your buddy. Due to the underdeveloped social skills of the group (in their youth) and lack of conventional social mores, they probably slept with the out gay one. Every geeky group has at least one slutty gay kid because, hey, who else sleeps with these guys in high school? Trade all around! Remember that kid with Asperger's who would always say the exact wrong thing at the most inopportune moments? Oh yeah, he was friends with the gay geeks. Those kids who played *Magic: The Gathering* at lunch? They were friends with the gay geeks. What about the ones who played live action role-playing games? Yes—them too.

Another peculiarity of gay geeks is their taste in fashion. If you can get by with a hot boy who loves programming, t-shirts, and only showers once every few days—you're in luck! For those who think the late 1990's baggy clothing fad is a thing of the past, then meet a few geeks. While hipsters parade around in the high fashions of some given time period, geeks wear the most common clothing from ten years later. Hawaiian shirts! Baggy pants! Silly Hats! Carry a few ten-sided dice in your pocket, learn the rules to *Settlers of Catan*, grow a beard and you're in! Not all gay geeks dress poorly, though—someone has to be the best dressed at the LAN party.

Remember, however, that strange and nerdy as many of their habits may be, there are numerous benefits to hanging out with the boys who make geekery fabulous. Being a geek confers outsider status, which is a strong predictor of camp—the humor of outsiders. In addition, the most noticeably fashionable geek decorating style—steampunk—mixes Victorian decorating sensibilities with technology, making streamlined and boring machinery look positively gorgeous. Fashion aside, one of the critical points of the geek social code is loyalty. Until someone points a gun in a typical young geek's face he will not change his friends (or his shirts). Geeks are more married to their good friends than any other group of people (except possibly singaylaritys). They're also more than willing to come over and help set up the wireless router—the modern porn plotline equivalent of the plumber and the housewife. "Oh sorry, I put the router under the table. Mmm-hmm…down there."

Dates: bohemian geeks, bears, leathermen

Tricks: anyone willing, but most likely exposed to other bohemian geeks and bears

Avoids: anyone non-geeky, everygays

Native habitat: the comic book store, Silicon Valley

Bears

Primary Humours: filth, divinity

Bears are hairy, husky, oft-bearded gay men who revel in the tropes of working class masculinity and stand at the opposite end of the spectrum from twinks. Bears are also mostly middle-aged, but these aspects belie the reason they band together. You see, when bears were younger they were often still rotund and furry. At the time, however, their peers were still lithe and smooth. They found they lived entirely outside the confines of what gays stereotypically consider "attractive." So they formed their own community.

Bear culture grew as an offshoot from leather culture. During the heyday of the hanky code, a system of placing colored handkerchiefs in your back pocket to indicate various sexual proclivities, some people started putting little teddy bears where they would normally indicate their love of fisting or shrimping[1]. The notion took off and it became quickly apparent that there was a whole subculture ready to explode. Soon after, The Lonestar Saloon opened in San Francisco promoting bear publications and selling bear schwag and the scene quickly grew. It took time to evolve into the butch drag it is now, of course, but extra weight and hearty body hair were included from the beginning. Grr.

The prevalent bear image is heavily informed by contemporary ideals of "normal" masculinity and, if a bear does his job right, he is entirely indistinguishable from his middle-aged heterosexual counterpart aside from his superior taste. Looking and acting masculine is an integral part of bear culture and it is taken quite seriously. Bears are guys who just happen to, ya know, suck cock. Their presentation, while seemingly heteronormative, is in actuality fairly subversive. For one, they eroticize hair, fat, and middle age—all serious no-nos in youth-obsessed mainstream gay culture (and mainstream hetero-culture for that matter). In addition, they act out against the cultural perception that all gay men are feminine. Peter Hennen, author of *Faeries, Bears, and Leathermen*, argues bears essentially divorce femininity from homosexuality.

By now, bear culture has evolved its own massive party circuit with events at every gay vacation town and each year events look more like a fatter, hairier, circuit party. They also have local

---

[1] Shrimping is sucking someone's toes.

chapters in most urban areas, though they'd rather be in the forest to be sure. There are few subsets of bears worth noting:

Muscle Bears

A distinct subset of the bear, muscle bears are huge, sometimes bearded, hairy dudes who are muscle-huge rather than fat-huge.

Otters

Skinny, hairy participants in bear culture.

Cubs

Young guys who have guts and beards and follow bear culture. After they turn thirty-five they become bears.

Polar Bears

Old bears with white hair.

Dates: bears, leathermen, bohemian geeks

Tricks: bears, leathermen, bohemian geeks, muscle boys, sometimes twinks, or trade for variety

Avoids: no one—they're far too jolly to be avoiding people

Native habitat: gay campgrounds, bear weekends at various vacation towns, bear bars

Leathermen

Primary Humours: filth, glamour

Leathermen take machismo to such extreme levels even bears get intimidated. Although no daddy worth his weight in chains would admit it, full leather daddy personas are a form of hypermasculine drag. Their ever so careful posturing—which is so very important for the culture to function—is still an act. There are no heels or makeup, but there is infinite posing and look giving.

They give reads with a cat-o-nine-tails instead of salty statements and they wear leather instead of lamé, but the underlying artifice of their characters are two sides of the same coin.

It is, of course, perfectly fabulous that they engage in such wild distortions of masculinity, but it is a seriously complicated game. Leather tops cannot have lisps. Leather tops cannot engage in feminine behavior while in character. Leather tops cannot display non-masculine emotions in character. Leather bottoms have a somewhat wider berth of character traits available, but they are equally constrained by rule sets and their subservience to the tops.

There is much discussion in the leather community regarding the current rules and degrees of discipline required for participation. The two basic groups—old guard and new guard—pull the culture in vastly different directions. Old guard leather groups first spawned after World War II when there were huge quantities of young gay guys who felt lost when peacetime began for they thoroughly enjoyed the discipline and bonding associated with military life. They coalesced about the same time as the first motorcycle clubs and their respective styles long borrowed from one another. There was an extremely complicated training system by and for tops. A top learned the ropes using tools of violence, control, and by honing their own behavior. After training was complete, a freshly promoted master would perform a public flagellation of a slave for all the other masters to watch.

Younger generations often find the level of effort required to become an old-guard top prohibitively difficult and have lost much of the cultural zeitgeist that spawned the original groupings (old guard leather became popular in the 1950s). They believe in leather more as an agreed-upon post-modern sexual conversation between partners. The old-guard style still exists, certainly, but as time passes there are increasingly disparate amounts of discipline, torture, or even clothing required across the diaspora of leather groups. It is worth noting that most practitioners of leather culture are near or above forty.

If you want to meet the local leather group or other severe kink enthusiasts there are a few places to start. Search for a local "munch" or kinkster dinner party. Most cities have one and a quick search turns them up. There are sometimes local groups even in relatively remote areas. In addition, most large cities have at least one leather bar—often the same bar the bears go to.

A note of etiquette: if you are amongst leathermen and you see a man in a collar with a nearby man who seems to be his master it is considered impolite to speak directly to the slave (the collared one). You should greet the master first.

A note of fashion: a collar is not simply a charming leatherman's fashion accessory. It is a symbolic ownership of and submission by a slave. If wearing a fashion collar, be mindful of its meaning.

Dates: leathermen, bears

Tricks: those willing to engage in power exchanges

Avoids: people who pursue equality in the bedroom

Native habitat: The [insert the nearest major city's name] Eagle

Furries

Primary Humours: filth

Furries, not to be mistaken for plushies or people who eroticize being stuffed animals, are a large, mostly gay subculture that take on animal avatars. They like to pretend, at least officially, there are straight furs. There are, but they are a serious minority. Furries are among the most paranoid of gay subcultures—until very recently they had fairly strict rules about press at their major events.

Furries have an extremely well-developed culture with its own artists, internally well-known participants, and infamous scenesters (Mecha Wolf being among the most impressive). There are stereotypes associated with various animals: foxes are slutty, dragons are pretentious, horses are size queens, etc.

Although it often goes unstated, furs are indeed a part of gay culture and chances are you know one. Attending a furry convention—especially Anthrocon in Pittsburgh or Further Confusion in San Jose—is like spending a weekend on an acid trip.

Dates: furries, bohemian geeks

Tricks: furries, bohemian geeks

Avoids: anyone involved in the gay scene

Native habitat: Second Life, Anthrocon, Further Confusion

Twinks

Primary Humours: divinity

It is unfortunate so many young gays are misclassified as twinks when they aren't. Everyone is youthful for a while and it's hard to look bad when you're young. When gays are teenagers (14-17) they are called chickens and then, if they value appearance above all else they will become twinks upon turning eighteen. My advice: twink is not a great thing to be. Both revered and reviled due to their youth and their looks, twinks are the avatars of gay culture's youth worship. The gold standard of delicious twinkdom requires:

Youth

A rock hard, gym-hewn body—slim, not bulky

Sparse, soft hair across the chest or no body hair

No facial hair

Knowledge of these assets

You see, twinks get their name from the massively fake twinkie snack cake. It's empty calories, mostly air, and filled with cream, just like these boys. It is possible to be a twink with darker colored hair, eyes, or with a modicum of closely trimmed body hair, but any deviation from the standard gets the bearer demerits. Twinks cannot be ugly. Not that there's a rule—it simply is not possible.

Twinks represent the most common gay male appearance fantasy—the zenith of hotness. Many gay males in their twilight years remember their late teens and twenties fondly and the twink stands as the totem for recalling good times. A twink generally despises anyone even a slight rank of hotness lower than himself and causes tidal waves of masturbatory fantasies in his wake. They can often be spotted at the most popular club in town dancing without a shirt on. They probably have at least one absurdly attractive friend in tow and are not generally assumed to be monogamous.

Twinkdom begins to fade around age twenty-five, but can last until thirty for the especially well preserved. As the unsustainable youthful good looks of the twink gather crows feet, larger pores, and general signs of age they start to freak out. A true twink coasts mostly on his looks, and may suffer a severe crisis as they fall out of the bubble where everyone fought for their attention. Of course, most people have developed their gay humours by this point, which softens the blow, but it's hard to lose your youth when it's your main selling point. Some people are hot their entire lives, but you cannot be a twink past your thirtieth birthday. Period.

If you are a twink and you plan on coupling, be sure to attract a hot mate by twenty-eight or so to lessen the pain of losing your youthful good looks. It is also to be noted that, due to the endless worship bestowed upon them by the community at large, many twinks are terrible in bed as they have not yet had to master any skills beyond having a pretty face. By thirty-two or so they are often skilled enough from their post-youth dark years to be worth a romp. Although I urge all beautiful, youthful gays to live it up, try not to come off vapid enough to be a twink—develop your personality now while people are unusually gracious and you can continue your fabulous reign well past your youth.

Dates: what's a date?

Tricks: other twinks, sugar daddies, scene queens, muscle boys, anyone hot

Avoids: "old" (one to three years older than them) and ugly people

Native habitat: their back, the club

Filth Queens

Primary Humours: filth

If you aggressively pursue sex with whoever suits your fancy and purposefully chat loudly about uncommon sex practices trying to horrify (or attract) eavesdroppers you might be a filth queen. Filth queens own up to all the dark fantasies inside them and present each as a fabulous, desirable trait. They often dress and behave in purposefully disgusting or offensive ways and engage in risky or at least highly unorthodox sexual practices. A notorious filth queen I know used to make t-shirts featuring gigantic, sequined cocks. It made his desires abundantly clear. One main filth queen goal: in particular, the reason they're so public about everything, is to shock and awe the tightly wound conservative and conventional gays.

Dates: filth queens, hedonists, scene queens, singaylaritys

Tricks: as often as possible

Avoids: assimilationists

Native habitat: bareback parties, after-hours clubs, bathhouses

Sugar Daddies

Primary Humours: glamour

Sugar daddies are older, richer gay men who pay for the attention and devotion of pretty young things. In exchange for time, attention, and affection, a poor young gay can come out well-fed with a new wardrobe. Although cross-generation relationships raise plenty of eyebrows, they are by no means off limits. Some younger guys want a "daddy" and exclusively date guys ten plus years their senior. Although assumed to be a primarily economic arrangement, these relationships have the potential to become long-term. Remember: many lads looking for sugar daddies don't realize how cheap some of their desires are, so the monetary bar might not be as high as you'd suspect.

Dates: twinks, drag queens, street boys

Tricks: with money

Avoids: anyone over twenty-five

Native habitat: buying drinks for the youngin's at the club

Street Boys

"Street boys/they never waste time/the only things that matter are love, sex, crime."

–Street Boys by DMX Krew

Primary Humours: camp, divinity

 Street boys are homeless young gay men—often disowned or runaways—who make livings as petty thieves and hookers until their careers in drag take off. Due to their dire circumstances these youngsters live each day of their lives with abandon and never look towards the future. They can make interesting company and can easily be plied with offers of free food. Want to do something fun? Find a stuffy art gallery opening with hor d'oeuvres and free wine and invite the local street boys out with the promise of a free meal. Your street boy friends get to eat and the art crowd will be horrified—it's a win-win situation!

Dates: street boys, sugar daddies, drag queens

Tricks: for money

Avoids: cops

Native habitat: the street, couch surfing

Butch Queens

Primary Humours: divinity, camp

Butch queens are extremely femme gay dudes that can *kick your ass*. They got beat up so many times as kids that they toughened up and do not take shit from anyone. If you call a butch queen a faggot they will walk right up and knock you the fuck out. Don't think their sinewy bodies prevent them from throwing a hell of a right hook. These guys are so high in divinity that they will present and defend who they are whether you like it or not. Butch queens generally come from conservative areas where even the pansies learn to fight. They make good friends and fierce allies.

Dates: butch queens, drag queens, masculine guys

Tricks: trade, closet cases, anyone butch

Avoids: bullies, perpetual victims

Native habitat: the bar

Scene Queens

Primary Humours: glamour, divinity

These are gays who go out all the time and know everyone. They make brilliant sport from what might otherwise look like drug addiction or alcoholism. If there are enough queens in your local scene, they will often get into a game of friendly one-upmanship. Consider the character evolution of Acid Betty, a New York drag queen: "My best friend at the time was a hairstylist, and we wanted to go out dressed up like freaks. It was a weekly challenge to try and make bigger hair, stranger makeup, and more absurd outfits." A large collection of scene folks continually compete to be on the best guest lists, befriend the most bartenders/door people, or simply get *noticed* the most. A scene queen's worst nightmare is being ignored. Befriend a scene queen if you want to get invited to all the best parties in town.

Dates: scene queens, filth queens, drag queens, butch queens

Tricks: anyone who will raise their social status

Avoids: pariahs

Native habitat: the VIP section

Perpetual Victims

Primary Humours: none

Perpetual victims are self-hating gays who miraculously make themselves into the victim in all circumstances. If they get sub par service at a restaurant, it's because the staff is filled with homophobic assholes. If someone doesn't like them, it's because that person *hates all gay people*. Did someone not compliment your scarf? They are clearly funneling money to anti-gay associations. Somehow, these are the guys who get nasty looks and their asses kicked by bigots, like, every day—even after leaving high school. They get stink eye ten times more than that and their self-esteem gets rebuffed at least a hundred times a day. They tend to project their self-hatred into their relationships and have appalling self-esteem. They do not seem to understand that consistently negative, self-destructive people don't make good company. If the perpetual victims were any more dramatic they would spontaneously combust.

Perpetual victims may come from a rough background and have a legitimately difficult life, but they can only see the negatives in life. Their divinity score is negative and they suck all the good feelings out of a room. If you find yourself bitching about how awful your life is every day at the bar and think everyone around hates you for being gay you probably should take a good look in the mirror and decide if maybe you hate yourself and are projecting that out into the world. Raise your divinity, dearies.

Dates: anyone else wrapped in sufficient self-hatred that the two can get into a spiral of mutual invalidation

Tricks: trade, closet cases, filth queens

Avoids: happiness

Native habitat: the bottom of a martini glass

Closet Cases

Primary Humours: none

Closet cases only interact with other gays in cruisy parks, adult bookstores, hookup sites and phone apps, or in clandestine encounters behind dumpsters. They are so petrified of dealing with their own homosexuality that they engage in extremely risky sexual behaviors and are generally bad for your health as a well-adjusted, out gay person.

Since they are so radically fearful of their own queerness they are terrible company to keep—they don't like gays except maybe when currently aroused by one. They react very, very badly when perceived or accused of being gay, but eventually have a serious breakdown and come out. The longer someone exists in this phase of gaydom before blowing open the closet doors, the more issues they will have later.

If you are reading this and you are a closet case, please consider coming out. We already know you're gay and we are waiting for you on the other side.

Anti-gay Politicians and Preachers

The most notable subset of closet cases are men who spend their whole lives fighting against gay causes, "curing" gay men at ministries, and denigrating gays everywhere only to later get caught in a gay sex scandal. There are so many instances: Ted Haggard, Larry Craig, George Rekers, et al. If a politician or priest spends his whole life trying to make life harder for gay people, there is a good chance they're gay and taking out their own self-hatred on those brave enough to come out. Each of these men is equipped with what is called the breastplate of righteousness. This is when someone engaging in clandestine gay sexual encounters portrays a front of being *super* conservative and supports policies that actively attack the thing they fear most about themselves.

Perhaps the best example is Peter LaBarbera, president of Americans for the Truth About Homosexuality. Peter, in an especially misguided habit, attends and photographs The Folsom Street Fair every year. He tries to get photos of men blowing each other and engaging in naughty nudity and then *posts the photos online* providing commentary on how disgusting they are. Peter is the gold standard of a truly broken closet case.

"Dates": women

Tricks: trade, closet cases

Avoids: exchanging names

Native habitat: sexless marriages, church, public office

Gay-listers

Primary Humours: glamour, divinity

Gay-listers are the richest, most influential gay men in town. These are the guys who own the houses on Fire Island and in Provincetown. They are well-connected, powerful, and advancing gay causes on behalf of the rest of us. With merely a raised eyebrow and an inclination they can buy and sell most people they come across.

Dates: gay-listers

Tricks: whomever they want

Avoids: the poor

Native habitat: jet setting, the red carpet, celebrity fundraisers

Muscle Marys/Gym Bunnies
(known as Chelsea Boys in the 90s)

Primary Humours: glamour, divinity

A Muscle Mary is a gym body obsessed man. They have developed physiques and possibly love the "juice." Although generally considered shallow, they are usually just really into weight lifting—they can be otherwise well adjusted. The concept of the Muscle Mary evolved from the Chelsea boy of the 1990s. During the 90s a particular stereotype took root in New York: hugely muscular queers who wore neon muscle shirts and competed with one another to become the most sculpted. Although no longer relegated to the New York gay ghettos, heavily sculpted queers still appear with great regularity in gayborhoods across North America. Especially hairy specimens may someday stop shaving and become muscle bears.

Dates: twinks, butch queens, femmy gays, because of the tireless competition of body fascism required Muscle Mary's never date each other

Tricks: other muscled men, dudes into muscle worship

Avoids: fatties

Native Habitat: the gym

Castro Clones

Primary Humours: filth, glamour, divinity

A rare breed today, this gay archetype once ran amok in the streets of San Francisco. In the late 70s and early 80s, a ubiquitous gay fashion trend emerged. Men started wearing fitted Levis, tight t-shirts, aviators, mustaches, and boots. So many people wore this outfit that it became practically the only way gays dressed in urban gay neighborhoods. Although the fashions were consistent, the essence of being a clone was more about looking and acting masculine rather than dressing a particular way, but there were certainly patterns. Clones were slutty popper addicts who, according to legend, continuously cruised for sex at the bars and baths. When the style went into decline some of the clone hyper-masculinity transferred to bear and leather culture. Clones have nearly gone extinct, but the truly dedicated gay-watcher can still spot authentic specimens in long-standing gay neighborhoods. *The Butch Manual* outlines everything needed to become a clone.

Dates: doesn't

Tricks: other clones, muscle bears

Avoids: commitment

Native Habitat: the 1970s

Stay at Homos

Primary Humours: depends on what they were before becoming stay at homos—staying home too often degrades glamour

If and when gays reach a certain age and/or if they get seriously attached or married they slowly convert from men about town to stay at homos. There isn't anything especially positive or negative about being a homebound queer it just happens to people at some point in their life. At a certain age staying out until the wee hours partying like a teenager gets perfectly exhausting and it's time to fill the planter boxes and tend to the garden. This is around the time dogs or children enter the picture. This type of gay is among the hardest to spot unless you join a community group or become an antiques queen.

Dates: other stay at homos; may be partnered already

Tricks: on the Internet

Avoids: midnight

Native habitat: the den

Well, now that you've been introduced to the neighbors, we should find the neighborhoods. In the next leg of our journey, we'll explore how to make your town gayer and where to move if you just can't make where you are gay enough.

Choosing a Place to Live

Some of you may be happy where you are. Others can't wait to get the hell out. Hopefully you'll learn a few tricks to paint the town mauve.

Life Outside Gay Neighborhoods

Most people think gay people live in San Francisco, New York, and Los Angeles. These places get all the press due to their queer density, but we have people all over the country. Don't think you have to live in one of the big three. If you find yourself living in a town or neighborhood that *seems* gay, but lacks queer density, it's probably just "artsy." There is an important difference between the two. There are plenty of places that are extremely gay friendly without specifically being gay. Although it is, of course, okay to live there, it's worth learning the few major differences. "Friendly" towns and neighborhoods don't carry poppers anywhere and might not have a gay bar, a bathhouse, a park where public shenanigans happen, or drag queen bingo games, gay libraries, community centers, gatherings, and parties during the summer including pride and "bear runs," or the many other items on the gay social calendar.

This doesn't mean you live in a doomed town. If you find yourself seriously bemoaning the area you live in consider the following:

1) It's gayer than you think. Stay where you are, travel when you can to the cities listed below and the events listed in the next chapter, and find non-gay ways to enjoy your town. If you're active enough in the local community you will eventually meet other gays. A 2003 UCLA Law School study by William J. Rubenstein, et

al, claims there is at least one gay couple in 99.3% of US counties. Unless you live in rural Nebraska, it is a near certainty there are other gay people nearby. So go out, explore your town. There are sure to be at least a few gays nearby. Find them and befriend them.

2)   Make it gayer. You have the power to change things. If you are out enough, live in an even remotely appealing locale, and advertise, you can start an event in your town. If Topeka, Kansas, home of Westboro Baptist Church (the infamous and reviled church responsible for the God Hates Fags protests), has gay pride events, so can your town.

I used to live in State College, Pennsylvania. It's a large town in a region often referred to, somewhat unglamorously, as Pennsyltucky. I'm sure you can imagine. This little town nestled in the mountains, thanks to its dedicated queer residents and extensive party culture, has developed a fully-formed gay culture. Over the past decade an entire scene has sprouted. There is now a punk rock drag troupe in town called the Clitorati who do odd performance-art-style drag shows. There is drag queen karaoke, travelling drag shows, and a large, entrenched, yearlong party circuit. A number of high-end club kids and drag queens in New York and San Francisco got their start there including Jane Lane, Peaches Christ, Hecklina, along with porn stars Matthew Rush and Spencer Reed. Is your town at least this fabulous? There really is no excuse for it not to be. If central Pennsylvanians can create a pansy oasis, so can you.

If you're starting from scratch and starving for gay company you do not require an expensive flight to San Francisco—it can happen in your town. Find a local community space willing to sponsor some gay event or do it in your house. Find local gays on your favorite social networking site and have a meet up. Find a willing bar and run a gay night. What's the worst that happens— you meet new people? Even if it's a flop at least a few folks will associate your name with lavender and forward gays in your direction. Just get out there and start something. Bitching alone in your living room gets you nowhere.

3)   Move (especially if you're from rural Nebraska). If you are unalterably miserable with the gays in your town...move. Just do it. Find a new job where you want to be, pack your shit, and high tail it over the rainbow. It is not nearly as daunting as facing a life of misery somewhere you don't want to be. Although you take your baggage wherever you go, moving from Nebraska to California will undoubtedly improve your quality of life.

Queers Are Always at the Forefront of Gentrification

It's not uncommon to hear the words "gay" and "gentrification" in the same sentence. Indeed, it's nearly as common to hear the phrases "Victorian" and "art deco" paired up with "gay." The gays continuously hunger for beautiful, derelict real estate. This, roughly, is the story of how the gay portion of gentrification operates: find any way-past-its-prime neighborhood with magnificent architecture. Move in, paint the house in gaudy colors and cover it in flowers. Other gays pass by and say "My, what a lovely house! Honey, we should pick up the terriers and move here!" And they do. They tell all their fabulous gay friends about this lovely, out of the way Victorian-through-art-deco neighborhood. Soon drag queens overrun the streets, men hold hands, people exchange blowjobs as barter for construction projects, and property values shoot through the roof! Beware: once this process is completed straights *with children* come in to prove how edgy and liberal they are. Gays took the trouble to nice up the place and then the straights, seeing how safe the neighborhood is, come in and ruin the whole party. They put up a fuss about the poppers-fueled backyard orgies, replace the mauve shutters with pale yellow, open straight bars, and otherwise blandly retrofit the place.

> Some Terms:
>
> Gayborhood—An urban neighborhood predominately populated by gays and lesbians.
>
> Gay Ghetto—A pejorative term for a gayborhood.

At this point, gay flight begins and another defunct neighborhood begins its gentrification. If you come across a nice-looking area, place your ear near the ground and listen for the sound of masses of reinforced stilettos skittering away. If that sound doesn't come, you will know it's still safe to move there.

Spotlight: Eureka Springs, Arkansas

Eureka Springs, a small Victorian town located in The Ozarks, has been recently conquered and is a prime example of the gays settling new territory. This happened many times in the past in other locales. Provincetown, Massachusetts, in particular, had a long history hosting queer artists like Tennessee Williams. However, the tale of Eureka Springs is different because of how conservative the dominant culture is.

It can be assumed there were always at least a few gays in Eureka Springs—most vacation towns, no matter how small, have at least one resident ready to suck the cocks of experimenting travelers. Curiously, Eureka Springs has many touristy Christian attractions including *The Great Passion Play*, a 1500-foot statue called The Christ of the Ozarks, The Living Bible Tour, a massive historical bible collection (including a first edition King James Bible), and more. It may seem that a heavily Christian tourist trap would be at odds with queer settlement, but there are a number of factors informing the queering of Eureka Springs. First, the aforementioned Passion play featuring a cast of hundreds has been running for *forty years*. Any town with such an epic, if dubious, theatrical tradition will have had queers in tow for a long time.

Indeed, this town is a perfect storm of queer gentrification: it has unique, beautiful Victorian architecture; it has a poetry festival; it has a writer's residency program; it has long-running plays; it has extremely rare antiques; and it has dozens of art galleries and high-end cuisine. It has practically every indicator of a gay town in the making. Thus, it should be no surprise that in 2007, the mayor, after coming to power with a major shift in the city council, passed a law allowing for gays to register as domestic partners.

The heavily Christian culture in the area flipped their shit and produced a documentary called *They're Coming to Your Town*.

This campy video, reminiscent of *Reefer Madness,* explains how the crazed and militantly gay citizens operate a modern day Sodom. Achieving the exact opposite of its goal, this grotesquely paranoid film produced a media storm that ironically turned away a portion of bible-thumping visitors while simultaneously informing gay travelers that Eureka Springs was open for gay business.

Current Queer Strongholds

According to *The Gay and Lesbian Atlas,* the ten gayest cities (with at least fifty gay couples) in America, with number one being the most gay, are:

1)   Provincetown, Massachusetts

2)   Guerneville, California

3)   Wilton Manors, Florida

4)   West Hollywood, California

5)   Palm Springs, California

6)   Miami Shores, Florida

7)   Decatur, Georgia

8)   Key West, Florida

9)   Northampton, Massachusetts

10) North Druid Hills, Georgia

In addition, the ten gayest zip codes (with at least fifty gay and lesbian couples) in America, with number one being the most gay, are:

1)   02657 Provincetown, Massachusetts

2)   94114 Castro, San Francisco, California

3)   95446 Guerneville, California

4)   94131 Twin Peaks, San Francisco, California

5)   90069 West Hollywood, California

6)   33305 Oakland Park/Fort Lauderdale, Florida

7)   94117 Haight Ashbury, San Francisco, California

8)   10011 Chelsea, New York, New York

9)   02118 Roxbury, Boston, Massachusetts

10)   77006 Montrose, Houston, Texas

It should be noted that Fire Island Pines (pop. 12) and Cherry Grove (pop. 15), the Fire Island gay resort towns, don't have a large enough year-round population to count in these rankings. Rest assured, they are very, very gay.

According to the criteria above, Provincetown, Guerneville, and San Francisco come on top as some of the gayest places, but there are plenty of other important gay neighborhoods, gay towns, and gay areas. They are broken into two categories: urban and small cities/vacation towns. Let's go through some of my favorites.

Urban

San Francisco, California—especially, The Castro (some Victorian buildings, mostly post-1906) and SOMA, or South of Market (industrial)

San Francisco is the gayest large city in America. For most of its history, SF was highly comfortable with vice as an industry and gay bars fit well within the greater framework of naughty inclinations permitted here. Then, during World War II, soldiers in the Eastern theater discharged for cock sucking got dropped off here. This huge influx of queers coupled with the already tolerant port city attitude brewed a perfect storm of homosexuality. San Francisco is the originating city of The Sisters of Perpetual Indulgence, a gay "nun" order/society. José Sarria, among the greatest drag queens who ever lived, started The Imperial Court System here in the mid-twentieth century after running for city supervisor in 1961. Talk about fabulous. Then, a few decades later, Harvey Milk picked up the torch and became yet another gay superhero from San Francisco. All the best 1970s' disco music came from here. The conception of the "bear" subculture came from here. All gay men should make a pilgrimage to this gay mecca at least once. During pride, an enormous pink triangle is set on the hillside overlooking the Castro. An entire pink mountainside—one can't imagine how San Francisco can get any gayer!

The most notable thing about San Francisco, compared to all the other cities on this list, is that queerness is thoroughly normalized here. People don't even notice gay couples holding hands or snuggling.

What shimmers: All of SF is gay! No one cares that you're gay.

What stains: The gays here are flaky. Everything is expensive.

New York, New York—especially, Chelsea (Victorian) and Greenwich Village (Pre-Colonial)

All of New York is gay enough to count. For one: Broadway is here with all the associated queer actors and dancers. Sure, there are millions upon millions of straight people around, but New York has a vast number of gays, a hugely influential gay club scene, and many gay cultural memes spread from this city. The 1990s birthed the "Chelsea Boy." A century prior, in the 1890s, gays started colonizing the baths as indoor plumbing rendered them practically irrelevant. Of course, with a long history as an important port city and a well-publicized fleet week it's no wonder New York and gay are nearly synonymous.

What shimmers: Lots of gay places spread across the city. Broadway.

What stains: Body fascism. The rent.

Los Angeles, California—especially, West Hollywood (art deco-modern) and Silver Lake (art deco/Spanish-style/midcentury modern)

When the film industry sprouted in the early twentieth century, there was a massive market for singers, dancers, and actors. Not surprisingly, gays flooded the city looking to become *stars*. This is the city where the concept of bodybuilding was introduced and the very queer genre of physique photography sprang forth. Amusing aside: the Los Angeles gay antique car club is called Great Automobiles of Yesteryear. In a town where everybody wants to be famous, there is a lot of glamour, a lot of camp, and a lot of gay.

What shimmers: Most of the Hollywood area is super gay. Everyone looks like a movie star. The eye candy is unbelievable.

What stains: You have to drive everywhere. Pollution.

Philadelphia, Pennsylvania—especially, "The Gayborhood" (Federal-modern)

There is plenty of old money and oodles of fabulous in Philly. The gay scene takes place in a handful of massive, multi-story clubs and bars. Philly also prides itself on its working-class appearances so there're loads of very masculine-identified Butch men around.

What shimmers: The micro-brew culture is amazing and Philly is the undisputed master of comfort foods.

What stains: Gay Philadelphia is a den of vipers. All of the gay places are *enormous* and impersonal.

Dupont Circle, Washington, DC (various architectural revivals)

The gays of DC, the ultimate company town, gather here when they're not infiltrating the US government. After all, there needs to be someone in the other stall when a closeted congressman starts foot-tapping.

What shimmers: DC gays are friendly. Super-touristy.

What stains: Every single resident believes they're doing something important and will stop at nothing to inform you of this. Super-touristy.

Shadyside, Pittsburgh, Pennsylvania (Victorian)

Pittsburgh, the supposed location of the American *Queer as Folk*, has plenty of interesting corners and Shadyside is certainly the gayest. It's a long way from the Liberty Avenue bars downtown in the strip district, but it has beautiful tree-lined streets. Bloomfield and Squirrel Hill catch gay runoff and the Mexican

War Streets make a decent effort to be queer these days too. But Shadyside is where it's at. Note: *Queer as Folk* was actually filmed in Toronto's Church Street which is described below.

What shimmers: The food, the glorious imperial architecture, everything is cheap, people are nice.

What stains: The gay areas are spread out across the entire city.

Capitol Hill, Denver, Colorado (Victorian)

Living on Capitol Hill means you get to stare at a gold-leaf rooftop each and every day. Few things are more decadent. Also, people are notoriously healthy and the whole place feels very neighborhoody. Once cars became popular, Denver gained acclaim for being situated about halfway across the country. A multitude of cross-country travelers including the queer-as-hell Beats stopped over in Denver now and again. In addition, the "unsinkable" Molly Brown (famous feminist *and Titanic* survivor) used to reside in Capitol Hill.

What shimmers: The weather is nice, the city is beautiful, everyone is healthy.

What stains: The locals are often standoffish with travelers. It takes a while for Denver to warm up to you.

Capitol Hill, Seattle, Washington (Victorian-early twentieth century)

Seattle's Capitol Hill is the best place to sit out the rain with a warm coffee and a hot companion. Up on the hill, you see beautiful Mt. Rainier on one side and the space needle on the other. Gays here are super-outdoorsy. Everyone is friendly and there are plenty of hiking clubs.

What shimmers: The gay hiking clubs, the coffee, beards-n-flannel.

What stains: The rain.

Lavender Heights, Sacramento, California

Lavender Heights has the best community resources for a city its size. There is a popular gay and lesbian center, a gay library (The Lavender Library, Archives, and Cultural Exchange), and plenty of other all-gay organizations. Everyone too normal for San Francisco moves here and starts a community group.

What shimmers: Community groups a-plenty, everyone is even-tempered.

What stains: All the outrageous people moved to San Francisco long ago.

Mt. Vernon, Baltimore, Maryland

Baltimore is generally so strange and so queer it hardly requires a special neighborhood, but it still exists! Mt. Vernon features prominently as the working neighborhood of Pecker's sister in the movie *Pecker*. "Hi Mary! Oh it's alright, we call everybody Mary in Baltimore." Residents of the neighborhood have a massive phallic symbol, the "original" Washington monument, to meditate on every day. And, of course, Baltimore is a port city.

What shimmers: Everything is cheap, everyone is friendly, the local color is unique.

What stains: Baltimore is the trash capital of America. Though that might be a good thing.

Savannah, Georgia

This beautiful city filled with Spanish moss and glorious pastel architecture has a large gay culture. *Midnight in the Garden of Good and Evil* greatly details Savannah gay life—even using local drag queens. A port city with delicious architecture and an enormous art school, Savannah's cup of gay runneth over.

What shimmers: The architecture, loads of "bisexual" art students.

What stains: The humidity is 100% all summer. You can't step outside without breaking a sweat.

Other Gay Neighborhoods

Jamaica Plain, Boston, Massachusetts

Travis Heights, Austin, Texas

Lakewood, Cleveland, Ohio

Burnside Triangle, Portland, Oregon

The Short North, Columbus, Ohio

Fruit Loop, Las Vegas, Nevada

NoDa (North of Davidson), Charlotte, North Carolina

39th and Penn, Oklahoma City, Oklahoma

Condado, San Juan, Puerto Rico

Oak Lawn, Dallas, Texas

Montrose, Houston, Texas

Carytown, Richmond, Virginia

Midtown, Atlanta, Georgia

French Quarter, New Orleans, Louisiana

Ft. Lauderdale, Florida

Small Cities and Vacation Towns

Fire Island Pines and Cherry Grove (both on Fire Island), New York

Cherry Grove and Fire Island Pines are the *original* gay vacation towns. The Fire Island gay party began, roughly, in the 1930s. According to local legend, the herald of the grand parties to come came when Christopher Isherwood and W. H. Auden showed up to a party dressed as Dionysus and Ganymede, respectively, carried on a gilded sedan chair by a group of singing followers. Ever since the wild early days, people have been shagging on the dunes and dancing in the sand. If there were one place to go in the summer, this would be it. The forested walkway between the two towns is a super-cruisey area known as the meat rack. It's a manageable ferry ride from New York City.

Provincetown, Massachusetts

Provincetown is a major gay town. It has a long history of artists in residence including Tennessee Williams and Eugene O'Neil and many current, important gays have homes here. Famous summer residents include John Waters, Marc Jacobs, and Andrew Sullivan. Provincetown has a plethora of festivals across the year including weeks for bears, dykes, and trannies as well as an important film festival. Provincetown is also home to a large number of Portuguese residents who have their own radio stations, restaurants, and bars in town. Grab the ferry from Boston and see whales along the way. If you want a fun filled faggy weekend go to P-town. The main strip is called "Commercial Street" and along this one street you can attend an afternoon tea dance with undulating gay bodies or walk across the street to the vegetarian restaurant maintained by lesbian Buddhist nuns. It's diverse, to say the least. Be sure to go to the Portuguese bakery for the best sweet bread you have ever had in your life.

Eureka Springs, Arkansas

Accidently popularized by a "focus on family" anti-gay film about gays taking over their town, Eureka Springs is one of the only gay resort towns in the Deep South. There is a very large Christian tourism industry in town. See above.

New Hope, Pennsylvania

New Hope has been filled with queers, artists, and bizarre boutiques since at least the sixties. Many of the local gay bars have closed, but there are still gay-owned hotels and Victorian fashion-clad drag queens parade down the main street on holidays. There is a store in town that sells Victorian birdcages, death portraits, and sideshow memorabilia. It's a must-see. Mostly visited by people from South New Jersey, the Lehigh Valley, and Philadelphia.

Guerneville, California

Nestled in the redwood forests of Northern California, Guerneville is along the Russian River in the middle of wine country. There are quite a few resorts here—some of them clothing-optional—and wild, weekend-long parties on major summer holidays. San Francisco is the major feeder city.

Rehoboth Beach, Delaware

The gays of Rehoboth are hidden in plain sight. There are plenty of gay bars and resorts, but the gay beach is well towards the south end of town. There is a long-standing house party culture here so it helps to know the locals. This is the main gay vacation destination for Southeastern Pennsylvania, Baltimore, and DC.

Palm Springs, California

This beautiful town in Southern California has plenty of lush golf courses and year-round sunshine. The police harshly cracked down on "vice" in 2010, so public cruisers be warned. Los Angeles and San Diego are the nearest major cities.

Asbury Park, New Jersey

Gays fleeing New York who didn't make it to the scenic Poconos landed here and turned this rather past-its-prime location into a brilliant resort town. It's mostly populated by Northern New Jersey folks.

Ogunquit, Maine

Populated largely by lesbians, Ogunquit is the hidden gem of New England. This small town gets some very decent talent in from New York and has plenty of beautiful scenery.

Northampton, Massachusetts

This small town north of Springfield houses a large—and thoroughly under the radar—gay colony. If you seek a town-as-open-air-gay-bar Northampton is probably not for you.

Key West, Florida

When Tennessee Williams wasn't vacationing in Provincetown, he was here. Key West is a charming island off the coast of Florida known for its beautiful weather, attractive men, and key lime pie.

Wilton Manors, Florida

This small town just north of Ft. Lauderdale is a preposterously gay vacation town near equally gay Ft. Lauderdale. Remember to pack some white linens when traveling in the summer as it gets hot.

Decatur and North Druid Hills, Georgia

These two towns north of Atlanta host extremely high percentages of gays. Due to the severe summers Georgia is best in the spring and fall.

Collingswood, New Jersey

Collingswood, an otherwise plain town, lies on the sole 24/7-train line in and out of Philadelphia. Older gays interested in homesteading settle here and then take the "party train" into the city for weekend adventures.

State College, Pennsylvania

State College has what amounts to a cult surrounding its collegiate sports teams as well as multiple gay clubs nights as well as a gay bar named Chumley's directly in the center of downtown. During home football games, State College becomes the third largest city in Pennsylvania, besting Allentown. Being a college town, State College also has vast swaths of hot, muscled eighteen to twenty-two-year-olds running about. This eternal party has raged continuously since WWII ended. Although it may seem an odd entry to this list, I lived there for many years and found the gay culture well developed and plenty of fun. There is a group of drag karaoke performers in town who are fully invested in the glorious camp art of karaoke.

Canada

Le Village Gai, Montreal, Quebec

Cleverly called the gay village, this is a great neighborhood for Francophiles looking for adventure in Canada. Nestled in the province of Quebec, home to the largest French-speaking population outside of France, this Montreal neighborhood is a perfect stop for poutine and high fashion.

Church Street, Toronto, Ontario

Toronto, the largest city in Canada, is gay in much the same way New York is: there are so many damn people there's bound to be a lot of queers. Many films and television shows are filmed here so actors abound. Additionally, those into the heavy Eastern Canadian accents might consider this neck of the woods. Gay Toronto knows what it's all aboot, eh?

Davies Street, Vancouver, British Columbia

This "official" gay neighborhood, politely vying with Yaletown and Gastown, is drowning in the famed BC bud and surrounded by beautiful scenery. Practically everything not filmed in Toronto is shot here.

Gay Flight

Have you ever heard of white flight, the opposite of gentrification? It's when the white residents of a predominantly white neighborhood flee to other places as other races move in. It doesn't take much—a twenty percent change in the neighborhood's race makeup can trigger a white exodus. There is a corresponding phenomenon known as black flight. In well-established gay neighborhoods a new phenomenon is brewing—gay flight. Straights, feeling comfortable in the oasis of flowerbeds and tasteful décor buy houses in gay neighborhoods and bring their breeder influences. Other breeders take notice and move to the neighborhood. After the straight-threshold is passed, gays start looking for the next big thing. Some may attribute this to the general class-bound gentrification process of pricing out poorer residents, but I much prefer the image of gays fleeing increasingly bland food and terrible floral arrangements. The antique stores shutter and are replaced with taxidermy shops. Currently, this phenomenon is happening in a variety of places in Urban American, pushing Philadelphia gays to South Philly, San

Francisco gays to Adam's Point in Oakland, and Chicago bears to Andersonville. Since gays keep fleeing to new neighborhoods, more straights—some with *kids*—move into long-held gay strongholds. Married-with-children-straights have been sighted with increasing frequency in Chelsea as gays flee to Hell's Kitchen. After sufficient straights move in the neighborhood, it stops seeming to be an appropriate place to casually cruise strangers on the street or have sex in the alleys and then more gays flee, calling out for Mary. There have even been rumors of straight couples buying houses on Fire Island. Is nothing sacred?

Making Money

Anyone can make money, but gays do it best. Although, of course, people have all sorts of reasons for the job they choose and they generally have more to do with availability and profitability than sexuality. What a sad state of affairs. There are plenty of gay jobs out there from the femme to the butch and everything in between. Anyone can snag a job, but only someone paying attention can get a gay job (or at least a *fabulous* one). But what makes a job gay? Is it something stereotypically gay people do? What if you're too butch to be a hairdresser?

Since it may be difficult to find a gay job or know a good line of work to cruise, I have identified

Job Spotlight
Carpenter

Carpenters come in many forms, but they all have one thing in common: they get paid to nail stuff. Maybe if you're lucky you'll get to put a hard hat on. Carpenters, essentially, build things using their hard wood. They may build houses, buildings, or furniture. The benefits of carpentry are numerous: plenty of sunshine and thus a tan, lots of exercise, masculine posing, eroticized working-class clothing in multitudes, well-worn boots, and a workplace full of other dudes. Remember: after walls go up in the house, there are plenty of places to sneak off during lunch or after-hours. Offer to give your new playmates an after-dark tour of the site and you'll have no trouble getting dates.

twelve major aspects of queer employment—the more aspects a job has the gayer it is. If you desire honest gay labor outside of standing in heels or lying on your backside, following are the queer gigs aspects and some example careers for each.

Attributes of Gay Jobs

Snappy Uniforms

"Sometimes the attraction to the uniform is so powerful in me that I feel as if I am making love to the clothes, and the man inside them is just a convenience to hold them up and fill them out—sort of an animated display rack."

--Tom of Finland

When it comes to looking good without having to think too much about it, little surpasses jobs requiring a uniform. Many uniformed jobs require tailoring, so it's assumed your outfit will look good. As an added bonus, a goodly number of people are uniform fetishists—they specifically seek out partners who wear particular uniforms. There is also a happily proscribed protocol for cruising uniformed men. Entire subsets of the leather and S/M communities ape police dress styles and many of these people just beg to get on their knees when you are in your work getup. No other type of work gives you clothing you can use to get laid. Is there anything hotter than the thought of sucking off a police officer, inviting the deliveryman in, or otherwise living out a porn plot?

Jobs with snappy uniforms: police officer, deliveryman, firefighter, military worker, priest, businessmen (suits).

Porno plot opener: the deliveryman arrives at the house. After getting a signature, he sets down the box and asks where he can put his package. His bulging shorts barely conceal his other delivery.

Growing Wood: green collar homos

"Green Collar" homos abound anywhere plants grow. There is the obvious job involving plant matter: the florist, but also the horticulturist and plant scientist. Spending even a few minutes walking around a research farm or nursery will find you rolling in gentle men tending to plants. Remember: someone needs to tend the shrubbery near the park bathroom.

Jobs involving plants: horticulturist, arborist, botanist, farmer, park ranger, florist, park cruiser.

Porno plot opener: you notice a sweaty, dirty guy bent over in the greenhouse. You express interest in his extensive collection and ask him what his favorite plant is. He responds, "Want to see my *Amorphophallus titanum?*"

Taste Masters

"My native habitat is the theater. In it I toil not, neither do I spin. I am a critic and commentator. I am essential to the theatre."

--Addison DeWitt in *All About Eve*

Let's face facts: all gay men think they have spectacular taste. As gays grow older, they find their youthful abs become harder to keep up and realize that perhaps it's time to gather a collection of interests and opinions on art, writing, theater, food, wine, design styles, or a multitude of other objectifications. It is nearly impossible to interact with gay society without believing, to some degree, in your taste. Over time, you get better and better and develop outrageous snobbery based around your impeccable tastes. At that point why not get paid to be a snob?

Jobs requiring cultivated taste: critic, sommelier, antique dealer, interior designer, curator, event planner, DJ, academic, archivist, being Joan Rivers.

Porno plot opener: a hot, young club goer begs the DJ to play his song. "Oh please, DJ, I'll do *anything* to hear my song." The DJ raises one eyebrow, cues the track, and delights that no one can see below his waist. The young club kid loves his four on the floor.

Job Spotlight
Lumberjack

Lumberjacks, Tom of Finland's original hyper-masculine obsession, have a special butch allure to them. After the end of a long day, a lumberjack is sweaty and covered in the leftovers of performing violence against nature. They tend to be far more muscular than other outdoor-workers and because they murder enormously tall life forms for a living, have a special gruff superiority. Nothing can be done to shake a lumberjack—not even working over their tree.

Social Graces and Charm

"I suppose society is wonderfully delightful! To be in it is merely a bore. But to be out of it simply a tragedy."

--Oscar Wilde

Perhaps because gays lie at a social intersection between men and women, and thus learn to communicate to both audiences while being a fully invested member of both and neither, gays tend to have a distinct knack for jobs requiring social graces. As a group, gays are drawn to jobs requiring perpetual charm. And we succeed. Since participating in gay society involves large quantities of men constantly attempting to out-fab one another, it is no surprise immense people skills emerge. With plenty of practice and using natural inclinations, socially-inclined gays aspire to the old epithet "slick faggot." If you are chatty, the life of the party, or a closet submissive then these are your perfect jobs.

Jobs requiring social graces: tour guide, restaurant server, bartender, public relations representative, promoter, event planner, drag queen.

Porno plot opener: a man walks into a bar, sits, and orders a drink. The bartender chats him up and after he finishes making the drink, he makes sure to brush the guy's hand for an extra second when handing it off. After his drink, the man mentions he has to use the bathroom with a wink. He gazes at the bartender as we walks into the bathroom. His keg needs to be tapped.

Escapism

Since the mascot of gays is the drag queen, it should come as no surprise that escapism is a major aspect of gay jobs. Stereotypical gay life centers around bars (escapist), clubs (escapist), musicals (escapist), the pursuit of camp (escapist), and continual fantasies about that straight coworker with the incredible smile (escapist). At some point in early life, many young queers are often subject to torment and feelings of "outsider" status sufficient to develop an extensive fantasy life. Turning this into a career is only a short step away.

Jobs promoting escapism: travel agent, drag queen, bartender, actor, flight attendant, cruise worker, bathhouse attendant.

Porno plot opener: an absurdly hot guy is flying from San Francisco to Honolulu. When everyone dozes off over the Pacific, this guy "accidently" finds his way into the kitchen where two muscular flight attendants are filling the drink cart. They spill a little milk.

Aesthetics

There is a very curious and unique aspect of gay culture that helps a taste for aesthetics blossom. In straight society, men play out mating displays for women and women for men, but neither reflects the other. In other words, men do men things, women do women things, and although they compete with one another, they don't often find the things they do attractive in the opposite sex.

However, when considering the gays, it is very much possible—even likely—that you can be attracted to people *exactly* like you. This is why bears mate with bears, twinks with twinks, and interior designers with interior designers. Having attractiveness meta-awareness triggers you to seriously look at everything with an inward and outward focus.

Jobs requiring aesthetics: artist, hairdresser, art gallery worker, fashion designer, interior designer, event planner, film director, photographer, architect, makeup artist, painter, musician, writer, furniture designer, graphic artist, wig maker.

Porno plot opener: a photographer is shooting two hot, shirtless eighteen-year-olds for an underwear catalog. After guiding them through a series of poses they all get a bit excited. The photographer finishes the shoot and the boys, disappointed that their erotic underwear adventure is nearing an end ask "Are you *sure* you don't want some more coverage?" As it turns out, he wants very extensive coverage.

Performance

Since, at some point, most young gays "act" straight, they inadvertently pick up the skills required for success as a performer. It is no surprise then, that jobs full of pretending are natural draws to the gays. Although our daily gay lives are not nearly as horrible as before and thus not requiring as much daily performance, it is still a common career path.

There are plenty of ways to "perform." You could pretend to be really turned on by your paying sex partner; delighted at how much your pupils are learning; encouraging people to come see your brilliant sideshow; etc.

Jobs requiring performance: actor, impresario, drag queen, aerobics instructor, children's television show host, figure skater, stripper, escort, conservative politician, gymnast, dancer, TV news anchor.

Porno plot opener: the determined yoga student finds he can't quite perfect upward facing dog and downward facing dog. After class, the instructor demonstrates how dogs run in packs.

Kitsch

Spending tons of time deciding whether or not things are awesome produces vast quantities of those that are not. When things fail heartily enough or fall so far out of vogue that they become hilariously outdated, they fall into the amorphous world of kitsch. Kitschy jobs require skills at finding the hilarious amongst the garbage time produces. Whether it's commenting on popular culture, being a hipster, or dealing in vintage materials, having astounding taste in the good of badness is very near the core of the gay aesthetic.

Kitschy jobs: "antiques" dealer (1940s-1990s), sideshow worker, Las Vegas showgirl, pop culture commentator, pop artist, hipster, made for TV movie writer/producer/actor.

Porno plot opener: two actors in a made-for-TV movie about gay people realize they need to practice their kiss scene. One proposes they practice somewhere private. They get the shot in one take.

Excuses to Look Good Naked

Gay men are notoriously shallow. You could fight this urge and become a smarmy bitch or accept it and make the pursuit of being hotter than everyone else your moneymaking endeavor. Straight people are capable of this work as well, but no one knows how to pick out acceptably revealing clothing to flesh out their physique quite as well as your fellow homos. Go hit the gym and get paid!

Jobs that will make you look good naked: personal trainer, aerobics instructor, construction worker, lifeguard, model.

Porno plot opener: a man is working with his trainer at the bench press. The bencher, lying on his back, sees straight up the shorts of the trainer who is spotting him. The trainer shouts "C'mon! Harder! Give me one more!" From his lying position, it's clear the trainer doesn't need anyone coaching him to get "harder."

Hypermasculinity

It's hard to say for sure if gay men pursue hypermasculine jobs in reality or simply as a stag film plot device, but either way the idea is firmly planted in, at minimum, every member of the village people. By this point, it's clear that not all the boys debarking ships during fleet week are looking for girls, so there's a market. Fleet week is the time when a vast number of naval ships dock in a port city for a week and let the sailors run amok. Remember: you need to do more than buy the costumes to actually do the work. If you are a lesbian, a lesbian trapped in a gay man's body, or are just really butch, these are perfect jobs for you.

Hypermasculine jobs: police officer, construction worker, carpenter, military worker, lumberjack, trucker, motorcycle mechanic, prison guard, rock star.

Porno plot opener: After an unfortunate embezzling scheme gone wrong a notorious porno star is sent to prison. The guard notices the guy is clearly stressed and needs a cigarette. Having recently acquired some contraband from an earlier bust, he lets the prisoner light one up and suck one down.

Vast Numbers of Female Coworkers

If legions of fag hags are in your future, then consider careers where men are in the minority. These jobs often require sensitivity, some "bedside" manner, and are generally considered lowly by holders of more butch jobs. By this point, much of actual bias against these careers has long since faded, but gender disparities are still present. This queer career aspect is especially well suited for femme boys: you'll be treated like one of the girls and surrounded by other gays and women. Any man who crosses your path will just assume you're gay so it's also an excellent way to make "friends."

Jobs where men are the minority: nurse, flight attendant, teacher, travel agent, hairdresser, librarian, restaurant server, telemarketer.

Porno Plot Opener: An inquisitive patron wanders into the library seeking instruction in Dewey 176. The librarian, normally rather restrained, realizes 159 is no longer in use and discovers new entries in 419.

Special Gay Careers

There are a handful of career paths relegated almost entirely to the gays. This is advanced level gayness—far beyond sifting through job descriptions looking for aspects, these gigs are all gay all the time.

Drag Queen

Being a drag queen is a lovely job and certainly profitable if done correctly—just look at RuPaul. The rules required for succeeding at drag are so complex and specific they require their own manual—one that covers makeup, hair, fashion, bitchiness, and the theatre of femininity. But the basics are as follows.

Doing makeup isn't all that difficult. Just practice, practice, practice! If you have makeup capable friends ask them for a demonstration. If you don't, look up drag queen makeup videos online—they're incredibly easy to find. In all likelihood, your initial performances will be far away enough that audience members will be unable to tell your blends are off.

In Baltimore, they have a saying: the higher the hair the closer to God. Adopt this idea for yourself. You need at *least* two wigs to get the proper height, if not more.

When you first start working as a drag queen, you will probably just lip sync for tips. Meet people and network around parties and you will develop a name for yourself. After you gain notoriety and respect around town—and you will because you are too awesome not to—you may be hired as a promoter or guest for a variety of events once your "draw" is large enough. Then you get money just for showing up.

Notorious drag queens have parlayed their draw into a variety of ways to sing for their supper. RuPaul spawned a huge recording career and numerous television shows starting as a New York club kid. Jackie Beat formed the band Dirty Sanchez and regularly does cabaret. The members of the San Francisco group Tranny Shack use fake blood *and* glitter to deliver absurdly shocking stage shows. Drag maestro Peaches Christ, a Tranny Shack alum, runs midnight movies in the summer and her first film debuted in 2010. Chichi La Rue is an acclaimed porn producer and DJ. Drag is not just clowning—it is an actual career path.

All else being equal, there is one piece of advice above all others that will make life easier: "Eyebrows are sisters not twins." When bemoaning your makeup and feeling there is no way to leave the house without washing off and re-applying your whole face, repeat that phrase to yourself.

Escort

Although escorts are often scorned as being petty criminals or marginally intelligent twinks with big dicks and bigger drug habits, there is actually a highly profitable class of prostitutes who get to be the glorious mistress of many rich people…one after the other. They have advanced degrees, brilliant conversation skills, and big dicks too. A top-notch, business-savvy escort in a major city can make more than $250,000 a year. There are three main skills required to be an escort: class, confidence, and discretion.

In order to make it to the top of the escorting food chain, you must first learn about the things moneyed chaps discuss: art, architecture, theater, highbrow gossip of the local city, and related topics. Make a point of cultivating good taste now while sucking dick for rent money so that thick-billfold people feel comfortable around you. It is entirely possible you will be asked to go out in public with your dates, so be sure to learn the required skills.

Confidence is required of you for a few reasons. This provides, most importantly, the inner strength to use condoms *all of the time*. No amount of money is worth getting AIDS. Period. Besides, involuntary "vacations" due to disease outbreak detract from moneymaking. In addition, if required to behave like a top, you will need confidence to tell your John what a pathetic faggot he is while you plow him.

Discretion is key for one main reason: dudes aren't paying out top dollar because you're just *sooooo* hot. No. They pay the amount they do to get you to shut the hell up about seeing them. Don't kid yourself into thinking that you make hundreds of dollars an hour entirely due to your skill. Nope—it's discretion. High-end clients could easily have their lives ruined by misplaced gossip, so keeping secrets is critical.

If circumstance or desire compels you into this line of work, be sure to find yourself among the upper ranks so you can more easily rationalize away the cons of courtesan life. A note: it is extremely common, upon meeting new people, to ask what they do for a living. Unless you're a punk rock girl, I would recommend coming up with a sufficiently vague answer or you will have some very suspicious back-peddling to do at society functions. "Freelancer," "socialite," and "actor" are all good choices.

On the bright side, working as an escort means gaining audience with many very rich, very powerful men. They might be businessmen, theatrical producers, closeted politicians, or other high-fliers. Meeting the gay powerbrokers will give you a chance to see what kind of people make it the top. They probably won't write letters of recommendation or dole out jobs, but you never can tell—there are instances where a John wanting a more permanent, mistress-like situation might give you a sinecure at the office. If you would like to learn more about the illegal world of escorting, check out the chapter called "Origins" by Kirk Read in *Nobody Passes*.

Bathhouse Owner or Worker

Since the gays are so very fond of sex, it is no surprise that nearly every major city has a bathhouse seriously raking in cash. The concept of the bathhouse is by no means new—public baths have existed for most of human history. However, as with most things eventually conquered by the gays, they were gentrified. As indoor plumbing appeared increasingly often in urban areas, the need for public baths drastically declined. Over the years fewer and fewer straight people went, but the homos kept showing up and then Poof! The modern bathhouse was born.

Basing modern businesses on structures evolved during the nineteenth century and before may seem curious, but their staying power indicates the amount to be made by them. For example, look to Peter Karlovich and Stephen Herforth. They own a bathhouse *and* act as fundraising party kings in Pittsburgh. They throw monster bashes on a regular basis with past guests including the mayor of Pittsburgh, Howard Dean, and loads of gays.

If being a political kingmaker in your city is not part of your master plan, consider becoming an entertainer. Although it's not nearly as common as it once was, some seriously important singers got their start at the baths. Hell, that's how Bette "Bathhouse Betty" Midler got her start *and* her epithet. Indeed, Barry Manilow got his start there too, accompanying her on the piano. Miss M. certainly was divine.

If you're sitting in a towel waiting the fifteen or twenty minutes until you cruise for another round of play, think about how many other people are there and how much they paid to get in. Add the extra cash for water bottles and the more colourful sundries, then the dollar signs will start backflipping in your brain.

The Gay Social Calendar

Remember when I told you that life gets better? This is where it really shines. It is critical to pepper the year with festivities because every queer needs a good celebration now and again. Gay events are critical to a sequined fist lifestyle because you tend to get laid at them, gays know how to plan a party, and they can make an otherwise dreary life more exciting. They can provide enough fun and excitement for one more year in your town, or a perfect reason for a getaway. There is something going on somewhere on Earth at all times. With careful planning and a little research, you can find an abundance of gay events near you and by attending enough you can meet like-minded queers. Gay events appear in small towns, in forests, in cities, and on the baseball diamond.

Many recently out gays imagine all of gay culture to be emblazed with rhinestones and festooned with feather boas. There is plenty of pageantry, to be sure, but there are activities and groups active during the year accommodating everyone from the most nelly queen to the butchest daddy and everything in between. Gay rodeos have drag events, for example.

The stereotypical haters and gay culture non-believers say something like this: "when I came out there was nothing for me. I am, you know, a totally normal guy who just *happens* to be gay. I'm not a queen or anything and I couldn't find people like me at the bars and clubs. Then I found [insert favorite gay activity] and now everything's different." These unfortunate gents are unaware that gay life spans the gender continuum, that gay rugby teams and theater fill their ranks with equally hungry cock suckers, and the homo rainbow of events can cause one to break a sweat, increase alcohol tolerance, or include appreciation of art. Sometimes all at once.

Pride

Gay pride is important to help you feel as fabulous as you really are. In a world attempting to fill gays with shame, it's nice to have a space where everyone gets together and says, "Fuck you. We are fabulous." Misguided straights may ask why there isn't a straight pride, but they don't realize that *every day* is a straight pride parade. Movies, books, television, and all other media celebrate the lives of straight people. Fortunately, we have our own day to showcase the wonders of queer culture.

Nearly every town with gays has a pride festival. Pride events are traditionally held in June and not by accident. You see, on June 28, 1969 the patrons of the Stonewall Inn in Greenwich Village were tired. They were tired of frequent police raids, they were tired of being treated as well-below-second-class citizens, and they were, according to legend, mourning the death of famed gay icon Judy Garland (her funeral was that day). The police attempted a routine raid and the trannies, drag queens, and other clientele had, quite simply, had enough. A few drunk, angry queens fought back, trapped the cops in the bar, and began what turned into a three-day riot. Due to the litany of highly famous queers living in New York in the late 1960s the Stonewall riots got much better press than similar raid-resistance events happening in San Francisco and Los Angeles at the time. For example, upon visiting Stonewall shortly after the riots, beat poet Allen Ginsberg famously said, "You know, the guys there were so beautiful…they've lost that wounded look that fags all had ten years ago."

The next year on the 28th of June there were parades in Chicago, Los Angeles, and New York to commemorate the occasion. By the year after most major cities had a gay group, many of which planned gay pride events at the end of June. Over time, the celebrations grew and grew until there were prides all over the world. Thus, June is the standard pride month.

Your town probably has a pride celebration of some form. These are an excellent time to meet local queers because anyone who's anyone shows up for at least one event. It is worth noting that two types of towns have non-June pride celebrations. Most college towns celebrate pride in April or May while school is still in session. Many cities with especially brutal summers, like Phoenix, hold pride during more seasonable weather.

Camping

Gay campgrounds pop up in surprising locations not served by more conventional urban faggotry. They are scattered across the entire country and are popular destinations in more rural areas. In areas lacking a major urban gay presence, campgrounds act as a seasonal gay town. Many of the campgrounds have permanent sites, the kind where campers have wooden porches. Many offer cabins for rent. Gay campgrounds are usually private and not visible from nearby roads and, as a result, offer great privacy for both the less out and wilderness inclined alike.

One of the most prominent and unique features of gay campgrounds is the dance club. Usually placed in a gargantuan shed or barn, there is often a DJ spinning all weekend. The less family-friendly among the grounds have special play spaces and many of the campgrounds are clothing optional. Be sure to call ahead before planning a trip to the nearest location as there is generally at least one family weekend (no play spaces), a lesbian weekend, and a bear weekend at most camps. Although these are all vital celebrations, those not into the themes will be heartily disappointed by children, tits, or fur. Gay campgrounds generally open shortly before Memorial Day and close right after Halloween so they have a lengthy, naked, sweltering camp season.

Gay Sports Leagues

For those still not convinced that there is a fully gay parallel universe, consider the plethora of gay sports leagues. There is a gay world series, a gay superbowl, and a gay games (formerly the gay Olympics), among other things. Whether reliving glory days or playing out jock fantasies, there is a league for you and other dudes like you. Many players identify as "masculine" and there is quite a bit of we-ain't-no-pansies attitude from some participants, but there is plenty of camaraderie and exercise nearby. Gay softball is by far the most festive of the groups, with their World Series booked end to end with parties and a huge number of competing teams.

The biggest controversy in gay sporting is the Montreal debacle of 2006. The gay games were supposed to be held there, but there was a drama-filled argument that quickly spiraled out of control about the venue size. Gays, being size queens by nature, re-awarded the games to Chicago. However, the Montreal games still happened. They formed a new organization called the Gay and Lesbian International Sport Organization. They host the OutGames and promote the global development of queer sports leagues in general.

Rule of thumb: if a sport exists, there is a gay league system.

Softball

Gay softball is played across the US and Canada in leagues run by NAGAAA (North American Gay Amateur Athletics Association). Most populated places have a league, save for Montana, Nebraska, Wyoming, and other mostly uninhabited or over-wintered locales. There are thirty-seven leagues and they gather each year in a host city for the Gay Softball World Series.

Football

Gay football is sponsored by the National Gay Flag Football League and culminates in the yearly Gay Superbowl held each Columbus Day weekend in a differing host city. Remember to place your flags on your backside *just so* to make sure the opposing team feels how hard you've been rocking the elliptical. It might even get you a date. You might even be able to sack the quarterback.

Soccer

Gay soccer, run by the International Gay and Lesbian Football Association, hosts tournaments and teams across the globe and has teams face off as part of the gay games. Just like parallel, global, town-based soccer, it is way more popular outside North America than in it, but teams certainly exist. Besides, who could resist a pickup game of shirts vs. skins?

Rugby

Gay rugby is popular in England, Canada, and the USA and is run by the International Gay Rugby Association and Board. Every other year the rugby teams compete in The Bingham Cup, the international tournament for queer rugby players. Gay rugby leagues feature the bulkiest and butchest gay sports players on Earth.

Basketball

The gay basketball circuit, managed by the Lambda Basketball League, culminates each year in the National Gay Basketball Championships. Be careful not to let anyone dribble on your chin.

Small Town Excursions

Queer vacation towns pop up in the most unlikely of places. Even many not explicitly "gay" are extremely gay friendly and can make for a delightful weekend. Getting out of town, even on a short trip to a nearby small town, is a great way to meet some new people. If there are at least a few art galleries, hip coffee shops and restaurants, and at least one "organic" grocery store, you are probably in gay-okay space. Though the local chamber of commerce rarely advertises overtly gay activities, almost all gay small town events have some form of Web presence. Check out the happenings before settling into a bed and breakfast and delightfully quaint happenings will follow.

Urban Adventuring

Nearly every city in the country has an indigenous gay culture with its own charms and personalities. They have their own events calendars and their own special days: Miss White Trash West Virginia in Morgantown, WV comes to mind as a stellar regional example. It is a common misconception that all gay-friendly vacations must happen in the big five (NYC, SF, LA, Provincetown, Fire Island). Gay culture is all around you and, for those inclined towards stay-cations, a critical realization. Search the Web sites of the gay bar in the city nearest you. If the city is large enough (more than 200,000 people), the bar is probably located near other gay restaurants, coffee shops, and drag show venues. A few nearby gay businesses and maybe a gay and lesbian community center populate these mini-gay-neighborhoods and they're a perfect place to find the local queer weekly and plan some must-see stops. The staff at most of these spots will point you where you need to go and a nice planning cocktail will ease the process. The notable exception is the [insert your city] Eagle, present in most cities, often located in someplace just seedy enough to feel dangerous and thus masculine-sexy. The Eagle is a leather/BDSM/bear club. The one in New York offers free haircuts once a week—you have to sit on your hands and get what they give you, but hey, they're free!

Circuit Parties and Tea Dances

Although considered retro by current standards, circuit parties and tea dances were once held in the highest esteem—both figuratively and due to the immense quantities of K, GHB, ecstasy, and other club drugs consumed. A circuit party by itself is a massive dance with a simple theme (black, white, etc.) that lasts for a whole weekend and often located in either a major city or decadent vacation destination. During the nineties, enough of these huge dances appeared across several cities that they became known as the circuit. Remember, this was the time raves were popular. Attendees of numerous parties became known as circuit boys both for their frequent attendance and stereotypical appearance: young, bleached, lithe, muscular, high, hairless, and barely clothed. Although the popularity of the circuit has greatly waned, a few of the greatest parties still happen annually.

Tea dances, not to be confused with tearooms, are dances that start in the early afternoon (tea time) and last until the wee hours. The major ones today happen around major gay party weekends across the country with Ascension at Fire Island Pines being among the largest. They are a regular Sunday feature in San Francisco for those who never went to sleep Saturday night and just aren't ready to part with the weekend yet. Both circuit parties and tea dances only happen in major gay locales.

Halloween

Halloween, also known as gay Christmas, is the sole time of year it's acceptable in conventional society to run around in preposterously slutty outfits or bejeweled dresses with three-foot hair. It would be a tragedy if gays were to forget the one day of the year they can cover their rock-hewn abs in colored, body glitter and paint the town lavender. Chances are your local gay bar or gay social scene has a massive Halloween party—possibly one of the biggest parties of the years; it's social suicide to ignore the call of the masquerade balls.

The Gay Rodeo

Perfect for anyone who absolutely *means* it when they call themselves butch, the gay rodeo circuit has events across the US and Canada. The rodeo finals are held every October in a different city. Many of the best contestants come from Alberta, home to the Calgary stampede—one of the world's largest rodeos—although rodeo groups exist in somewhat lesser cowboy-culture locales such as Florida. The gay rodeo is fairly similar to its heterosexual equivalent, but has a few special events unseen in conventional rodeo. For starters, they host the only women's bull-riding events.

If watching ladies fall off an angry cow isn't your idea of a good time, other special events are much sillier. The first gay-specific event is the wild drag race. The race begins with a team of three: a boy, a girl, and a drag queen. The three pull a roped calf across a line some distance away. Then, the drag queen mounts the calf and rides it back across the line. Many a wigged queen eats dust riding these calves. The second is goat dressing in which a team of two men attempt to put underwear on a goat.

Between the camp events and the regular rodeo competitions, the gay rodeo, if nothing else, is a great place for an entertaining date. There certainly isn't anywhere else you can see a drag queen ride a cow.

The Imperial Court System

Founded in the early 1960s in the United States by Jose Sarria, a queer so notable he has a street in the Castro named after him, the court quickly became known for its philanthropic and party-throwing prowess. Sarria had, by this point, become the star of famed San Francisco gay bar The Black Cat and ran for San Francisco City Supervisor decades before Harvey Milk, so this was a natural and permanent extension of Jose's queer activism and local notoriety.

The court is a fundraising drag organization with a massive coronation party where an emperor and empress are elected each year. These elected figures are responsible for hosting an endless succession of fundraising events that make them the second biggest LGBT fundraising organization in the country (after the Metropolitan Community Church). They are popular in most metro regions in the West, not as much out East. The most famous of all coronation events is the Night of a Thousand Gowns in New York City, though many smaller cities have their own community-driven events.

The Sisters of Perpetual Indulgence

The sisters, the habit-wearing order of gay society with possibly the greatest pun-name in the history of faggotry, help host major events on the yearly gay calendar. Their home base is in San Francisco, but there are chapters across the globe. The sisters dress in white face makeup and wear habits—their style is unmistakable. Sisters all have wonderful names like Sister Phyliss Witha Lighta-Day, Sister Porn Again, and Sister Bea Attitude. For all the camp of their getup, they are deadly serious about community service and the path to becoming a sister is a long and difficult one. It takes three years to proceed from normal human to sister. Aside from their more conventional service activities and colorful history—filled with pom-pom routines and AIDS crisis awareness raising—they run bingo nights and operate as security at all the most important San Francisco events (The Pink Party, The Folsom Street Fair, etc.). Be where the sisters are.

Bear Runs

Although a largely urban scene, bears tend to have gatherings in rural places and vacation towns with gay resorts and campgrounds. A bear run is when bears from a geographical area converge somewhere for a summer party, and a "run" is an old term for driving en masse on motorcycles. Almost all gay resort towns have a bear run and they are spread wide across the country from Portland, Maine to Portland, Oregon. If you have any affinity towards bears or at least look the part, it's an easy way to meet other gays without moving to a massive city.

Mr. Leather Competitions

Many smaller cities with any bar-based leather culture throw a Mr. Leather competition. These winners compete in larger feeder pageants over the year and the winners venture to the International Mr. Leather competition in Chicago every May. Many of these same people can be found at Mid-Atlantic Leather, the other major leather event. Even in relatively small cities, there is a leather culture and they often gladly accept new recruits. If you find a nice old-guard group, they might even train you. How very lucky you are. Bring cigars.

The Hit List

Want to know the biggest parties in the annual social calendar? Following are the largest and sometimes strangest gay parties on Earth.

Rio de Janeiro, Gay New Year's Eve

Start the year off right in Brazil during Rio de Janeiro's Gay New Year party. This epic festival draws jet-setting queers from across the globe together to ring in the New Year surrounded by impossibly beautiful Brazilians.

Night of a Thousand Gowns

This über-glam ball, held during the coronation of the Imperial Court of New York, brings together the New York gay-listers together for an impressive and very black-tie affair.

International Mr. Leather

This contest, held every May in Chicago, gathers the winners of worldwide local leather contests together for a huge convention-center-sized competition for the title of International Mr. Leather. There are a variety of vendors and all the key players of the leather and bear communities. Though they perennially host, no one from Chicago has won the title.

Gay Days at Walt Disney World

About as corporate as gay holidays get, gay days at Disney World is not an "official" Disney event, but it is massive all the same. Tens of thousands of revelers head to Orlando in the beginning of June for a week of dances and Mickey Mouse overload.

Gay Games

Essentially an Olympics for homos, this massive sporting event is hosted once every four years in a different host country. It used to be called the Gay Olympics, but apparently, the "real" Olympics have trademark rights to the name. Oops.

Dance on the Pier

The crown jewel of the New York Pride experience, the dance fills up an enormous pier with sweaty, muscled revelers who dance the day away shadowed by the Manhattan skyline. The lesbians have their own pier party nearby.

Gay Mardi Gras

Sydney's June pride festival, which has no relation to Catholicism or even Tuesdays, is considered one of the wildest in the world. Though residents of San Francisco or New York would vehemently disagree, Sydney is the place to be for pride. The city fully embraces the festivities and Air New Zealand has previously chartered a party plane—complete with fake eyelashes and a giant feather boa on the plane—to fly between San Francisco and Sydney.

The International Gay and Lesbian Film Festival

This pre-pride celebration in San Francisco carries the best new queer films and is the Sundance of homosexuality. It's full of cinephiles of all shapes and sizes and, because everyone watches the same movies, there is plenty to discuss (or swap) with strangers you meet.

Southern Decadence (Labor Day weekend in New Orleans)

Aside from being the final occasion to wear white pants each year, Southern Decadence is the perfect wrap-up event in the summer-heavy gay party season. Filled with all the "show us your dick" grotesquery expected of New Orleans, this gathering is as filthy as you would suspect. Pat Robertson, famed Baptist preacher and host of The 700 Club, claims this event is so sinful it caused Hurricane Katrina's rampant damage. Only New Orleans could hold a party responsible for the apocalypse.

The Folsom Street Fair

The Folsom Street Fair, held the last Sunday in September in San Francisco, and its companion-festival, Up Your Alley Fair, held the last Sunday in July, are massive S&M street carnivals. Up Your Alley, often referred to as Dore Alley after the alley/street it is held on, is considered the warm-up festival for locals. It's a smaller occasion with about 12,000 attendees and is less touristy. Folsom, on the other hand, has 400,000+ attendees engaged in a cultural celebration of BDSM and fetish wear. There are fundraising whipping booths, various violent activities, and myriad variations on vinyl, rubber, and leather gear both fashionable and functional. It closes every year with a massive Sunday night dance as well as a variety of pre- and post-parties. Even if you're not into leather, this event is so strange you'll think you're on another planet. *Everybody* goes to it and those not into the "scene" strut about in jeans and no shirt. Whenever religious groups claim gays are destroying America and show photos of outdoor bondage, this is where they take the pictures.

Fantasia Week in Provincetown

The largest and arguably most colorful major party of the year is Fantasia Week. Held in Provincetown every October, this throw-down in the extremely queer Cape Cod town is a celebration of transsexuals, transvestites, and drag queens. It's a weeklong living embodiment of Judith Butler's *Gender Trouble*.

Black and Blue Festival (Montreal, during Canadian Thanksgiving weekend)

Named for the inevitable bruises caused by this gathering rather than just the colors, this Thursday through Sunday party held every October during Canadian Thanksgiving weekend has theme nights for leathermen and fetishes as well as more generalized and less violent dance parties. Attendees aren't required to have festishized inclinations, as it's mostly an excuse to dance in play gear, but it certainly helps. It seems so very many major events on the calendar are hosted by the best disciplined among the gays.

Miami White Party Week (November)

Rounding out the year, make sure to head to Miami in November for the White Party week. That's right, it's time to dig into your "do not open before Easter" drawer and dress for a multitude of parties with the same theme: white. Filled with white clothes, white sand, and white drugs, this is a great way to relax before the holiday season drags you back to your local scene for the requisite winter events before jetting back to Rio to start the year all over again.

Getting Laid In Style

"...If every sexual encounter involves bringing someone back to your house, the general sexual activity in a city becomes anxiety-filled, class-bound, and choosy. This is precisely why public rest rooms, peep shows, sex movies, bars with grope rooms, and parks with enough greenery are necessary for a relaxed and friendly sexual atmosphere in a democratic metropolis."

--Samuel R. Delaney

"I know that true love is supposed to be companionship, growing old together, blah, blah, blah. I thought that was what friends were for, not sexual partners! Some of us want hot lunatic porn sex and we want it forever!"

--John Waters in *Role Models*

Tops and Bottoms

The ultimate in internalizing hetero-normative values, the top/bottom dichotomy runs rampant in sex discussions. Tops (insertive) and bottoms (receiving) carry thoroughly unneeded connotations of gender role in addition to indicating a sexual preference. Tops are seen to be masculine and bottoms feminine. There are plenty of cases where big, butch daddies love to get schtupped and there are very assertive, penetrating queens. Remember that utilizing these terms, in addition to insisting on unneeded gender, implies anal sex is the only sex one should wrap their identity in. When discussing other sex practices, like oral sex, people say, "I love to suck dick" rather than, "I'm a bottom." Try and move past these terms and use other concepts to anchor your sexual identity. If someone asks you if you're a top or a bottom, try responding: "I negotiate."

Picking Up Suitable Mates for an Evening

Glamour and divinity are essential talents to pull in the right evening companions. These skills, and the fruit of their labors, will help you cultivate and explore filth. Are you one of those guys who goes to the bar alone, sits quietly, and returns home alone (but don't like it)? Keep reading! This chapter is for when the goal is sex and only sex. This is not dating advice and should by no means be confused for it. Filth is required to do this successfully and enjoy it sufficiently. Otherwise, the post-trick experience will be one of shame. This is not the desired effect. It should feel good and last as long as it lasts.

One of the surefire ways to cultivate a sense of gay brilliance is to get laid. Often. By the hottest people you can find. There are many words for this activity, but it is commonly referred to as tricking. In order to get a tricking merit badge, you must do the following list of things. Remember: "sex" means any activity involving one or more parties getting erotic fulfillment together (often with an orgasm). This could include hand jobs, blow jobs, anal sex, or any other activity you equate to erotic fulfillment.

1) Have sex with someone you met that night at a gay bar.

2) Have sex with someone you met that night at a straight bar. Bonus points if you got him to ditch his girlfriend.

3) Have sex with someone you met in a bathroom.

4) Have sex with someone whose name you never knew.

5) Have scandal-causing sex and tell everyone about it.

6) Have sex with an eighteen-year-old when you're at least twenty-five.

7) Have a wild encounter with someone who seems meek and mild. Tell everyone. Bonus points if you figured out how wild they are before anyone else.

8) Have rough sex.

9)   Have the cops called on you because you're too loud.

10) Have sex with someone your best friend fucked last weekend.

11) Cruise someone in public.

12) Indulge someone in a fetish you've never previously considered.

13) Take someone's gay virginity or—better yet—fuck a straight guy.

14) Take a drag queen home.

15) Have sex with someone who owns this book.

Now, it's worth noting that these things cannot be done all willy-nilly. If you lift your legs without proper poise, you'll be branded a sleaze-fag and no one will want you. And that's worse than death or polyester. In order to complete the checklist of stories to horrify relatives in your golden years, tact and grace must be employed with the people, the location, and, most importantly, the timing.

In order to find a good trick, walk into your local gay bar or club and make a few rounds while pointing your nose ever so slightly into the air and making a genuine effort to look down on everyone who is trying to ignore your hotness. If someone looks you over from head to toe or smiles, look at them, give a coy smile, and keep on the rounds. There may be fifteen or a hundred more people who will do this, so it is best to case out all options.

After making the rounds and selecting the hottest person in the room, stand next to them and order a strong drink. Something that says: "I'm hot, wasted, and have impeccable taste. Getting into my pants is easy and fun." A martini or a Manhattan are perfect examples. Strike up a conversation employing the maneuver known as "assumed rapport." Imagine you've slept with them a number of times before and you are now playing the game of opening them again. By portraying a confident/divine vibe, you will score. Since practically everyone in the room was checking you out, it should not be too hard to assume this.

There are straight-identified men who secretly wish to indulge in homosexual acts. They may be closeted gays, or just have a very occasional hankering for some scruff and a stiff cock, but either way this is where you come in. There are also men who will never get down with you. You will figure this out quickly. Some of these men are hypermasculine and homophobic and they should be avoided. Proceed with caution. When trying to trick straight people be mindful that the rules are slightly different. They are not used to being cruised by men, so a bit more than furtive glances and (less, at first) cock grabbing is in order. First, remember to think of them by the proper name: trade. This is the title bestowed on all straight people who have slept with a guy or might in the future without internalizing a gay identity. In other words, most straight men are potentially trade. Enough with labels; let's move them away from labia.

In order to bed some trade two things must happen: you must make him vaguely comfortable around you and also let him know you are gay as blazes. If you are really femmy the second goal is probably already achieved. While hanging out make sure to engage in light and non-threatening touch—put your hand on his arm or shoulder while saying something. If he gets really uncomfortable or strongly jerks away and looks disgusted you should seek out a new conquest at this point. If he does seem comfortable, proceed by finding a reason to touch his chest, stomach, or some other part of his body—asking if he works out is a good opener to this move. If you hang around him for a while and prove you aren't going to publicly humiliate him with your faggotry (by getting frisky in front of the other straights) then you can pass him some excuse about needing to chat in private. After you have suspected that he's game, mention out of hearing range of others that you, in general, have had hookups with straight but "curious" guys, you think he's hot, and you would be fully discreet, of course. Make sure to mention that you think he's a good time and like hanging with him even if he's not interested. This provides both the ego boost of being sought after without the pressure of having to react to being pursued by a gay. Most trade need time to warm up to kissing, or never get into it, so keeping this a business-only venture will help you both get to the good stuff. To assuage some of his fears, politely inform him that dudes suck dick better than chicks and all of the other well-rehearsed lines from your high-school masturbatory fantasies.

Though a lot of trade like getting their dick sucked, some don't like having stubbly dudes sucking it. Indeed, they may harbor occasional fantasies of taking a shot in the mouth. If this weren't the case, the market for she-male porn would be significantly smaller. Ultimately, somewhere in the dark recesses of their minds, some straight men want a chick with nice hair, ample breasts, and a big dick.

If you would like to discover whether he wants to get or take it, shortly after you get on your knees and relieve his throbbing boner from his pants, and just before you start deep-throating it, ask if he'd rather suck your dick. If he would, he'll probably say yes. Otherwise, he'll just grab your head and shove it on his situation. Either way you win.

It is essential that you engage in these types of behavior. Vestiges of shame will make you an unpleasant name for yourself. All others may naysay your liberated behaviors, it's critical that you are having sex because you like it and it's fun, not to fill a void. If you only try to fill the void, all the wrong people will be attracted by your behavior.

...And Kicking Them Out by Breakfast Time

"What does a lesbian bring on a second date?"
"A U-Haul."
"What does a gay man bring on a second date?"
"What's a second date?"

Did you both get off? There's no need to let him stay any longer. After you both cum you have only two obligations: give him a towel to clean up with and show him to the door. You may find tricking to be a great way of making friends, but you still have no further obligation beyond fluid expulsion. Post-trick chatting can be awkward and disagreeable, so it's best to stand up and start dressing yourself after wiping the fruits of your labor off. Assuming you had an agreeable time, feel free to tell him this and, if appropriate, tell him to chat you up if you run into one another again. If you really felt you made a true, long-term connection, please disregard the rest of this paragraph.

I've heard of guys becoming good friends or lovers after casual hookups in bath houses, adult video stores, or even public restrooms. Most likely, however, the sex—and by extension, his company—will be mediocre at best and you should just say you had fun while giving him a polite yet empty smile. This is the universal signal for "I'm glad I got off. Now get out." When this happens to you remember that being kicked out has nothing to do with you and you should not negatively internalize it. It was just a trick.

Early in your career as a fabulous queer, you may mistakenly think you share a greater bond than an hour adventure, but this is likely not the case. It's rare that sex with someone is good enough to repeat. When you run into one another again, remember that he may not be as out as you. If he doesn't acknowledge you, try not to be offended; he may still be leading a double life and, sad as it is, outing people on the streets does more harm than good. Although, if you realize this is the case maybe it's best not to take him home again if he's warm in the bed, but cold in the streets. It's the twenty-first century—try and associate with other out people to build healthy sexual attitudes.

Additionally, try not to shit where you eat. If you sleep your way around town frequently enough, a rather terrible nightmare scenario will befall you at least once. While at a party, bar, or gathering, a large number of your former tricks may be in the same room at the same time. Although this is far from troublesome for some people, others become paralyzed by a living museum of former nights-of-pleasure. Beware.

A single caveat to the kick-them-out-after-they-cum rule exists: if it is Saturday night, your trick is especially delicious, and you are attending brunch with your friends on Sunday morning, keep your hot number over and bring him as a brunch guest. Your mates will be impressed and jealous at your tricking prowess and will seethe with rage that their night was not nearly as much fun as yours. Competitive gays make good sport of Sunday brunch dates but this relationship has a definitive end-time of 2 p.m.

The Ins and Outs of Cruising

There are a few places where you can get your rocks off the moment the desire arises. Wherever you go, you will be partaking in the age-old art of cruising. Cruising is the practice of walking around a specified location looking to get laid. Now. Without all the chitchat and drink-buying required at bars. Although the fabulousness of clandestine, anonymous encounters is debatable, it is most certainly efficient and it's best to know how to approach cruising so you don't get beat up or arrested. Black eyes and criminal records are most unglamorous save for a highly specific audience.

There are specific dos and don'ts for the most popular cruising venues and you don't want to be caught with your pants down (unless you do), so let's cover your bases to reach maximum exposure.

Parks

"Sometimes, on a really cloudy night, you wouldn't even know some guy was there until you touched him or he touched you. Sometimes nothing was said at all. You'd just hear breathing and the clink of a belt unbuckling."

--Tom of Finland

In previous times, park cruising was a staple of gay sex life, though it is certainly still around today. Most cities and towns—almost regardless of size—had a cruisy park area. It's usually a secluded and under-used area of the park. The Ramble in New York's Central Park is the model version of a cruising park section.

Park cruising protocols generally involve standing casually along a path or sitting on a bench until someone agreeable approaches. Direct men grab their dick through their pants and stare at the cruiser's junk. If he nods, smiles, motions towards the woods, or grabs his in return you know you're good to go. More subtle dudes may ask for a cigarette, a light, or engage in some form of brief small talk before motioning towards the shrubbery. Truth be told, it's the eye contact and the look of intent that gets the ball rolling. Although in many locales this is against the law, you might lead the fellow somewhere more private and just pick him at the park. Be mindful, since you are in a forest, not to get a terrible STD like poison ivy, oak, or sumac. Also beware of pickpockets—do not walk into an isolated space with someone who looks shady in a way that doesn't involve pulling their dick out for strangers. Some of the guys propositioning you in the park may be cops.

Bathhouses

Very few people go to bathhouses for a shower and a nap. Indeed, they are designed for sexual adventures. Every major metropolitan area has a bathhouse and unless you are hideously disfigured, it is almost certain you will get some play if you go to one at a busy time. The dress code is generally limited to a towel and shoes, but some venues have fetish nights—make sure to check the schedule lest you be caught without your leathers. Protocol is similar to parks, except many places have rooms that can be rented out for more privacy. Generally, non-logistical talk is discouraged, though meeting and befriending other bath goers is certainly possible. If a single person or group is in a room and they leave the door cracked open, you may peek your head in to get permission. A nod from the inhabitants functions as permission to enter. If you try to participate and someone brushes your hand away or otherwise indicates your involvement is not welcome, please stop. It is most impolite to get handsy without invitation.

There are two kinds of bathhouses: open spaces (sex clubs) and those with rooms (actual bathhouses). San Francisco is the predominant location of open-space "sex clubs" without privacy.

Peeps

Peeps, or "adult bookstores," have some number of semi-private or private booths that play porn with quarters or tokens—a veritable arcade of cock sucking. Politeness dictates that you should regularly put quarters in even when you aren't watching the films—the owners are nice enough to provide a hyper-exhibitionist space and mop your semen off the floor. Protocols vary per location, but in general leaving your door open, sticking your feet out under the booth door, or showing a hard dick to a passerby constitutes an invitation. Additionally, if there are no doors, making eye contact is generally thought to be an invite. This type of business is generally considered pretty trashy, sometimes outlawed, and generally on the queer fringes.

Public Restrooms

Cruisy restrooms, or tearooms, were once extremely common when being gay was outlawed and have subsequently waned as acceptance increased. To find a willing partner, walk to a urinal next to a potential candidate and go to the bathroom. Make sure to stand back far enough that he can see your goods. Check him out and play with yourself just a bit. If he responds, massage yourself until you both get hard—an erection is the only way to assure you're into it. Be very careful obviously staring at stranger's dicks in restrooms as straight people do not appreciate this forwardness. Fortunately, this is such a gross and willful violation of heterosexual urinal protocols that they usually just get uncomfortable and leave.

In many locales, under stall activities are de rigueur. Reading the stall walls is a good way to figure out if you're in a tearoom. As opposed to lame drawings or witty nonsense, stall walls often have e-mail addresses, telephone numbers, or other overt indicators of the goings-on. If you want to work a tearoom, first sit in a stall and pull your pants down. Start slowly and quietly jerking off until you're hard. If the person in the stall next to you is there for the same purpose, they are probably doing the same unless they're terribly shy.

Once getting yourself revved up, one generally signals interest. Your neighbor will do the same. There are a series of overtures where both sides of the wall indicate they're interested. After the complex signaling, whoever is getting serviced kneels to the ground and slides their dick under the wall where he gets blown, jerked off, or possibly penetrates an especially hungry and dexterous bottom. Many times mutual jerk offs are a possibility. When a receiving partner is getting stroked, he may place his hand under the stall and repeatedly squeeze his hand to indicate you should insert your hard cock. You may choose to do so—after some time an empty hand will retreat.

If a non-cruisy person enters the restroom participants quickly and quietly sit back on the toilet seat. Unsuspecting people hardly ever realize what was happening just before they entered. The players remain on the seat quietly stimulating themselves until this person either leaves or begins engaging in cruising signals. Popular tearooms often have an antechamber with sinks or a long distance between the door and stalls giving ample warning from hinge-squeak to intruder presence. Having sex in bathrooms is considered tragically retro and closeted by most of gay culture and is considered illegal in most contexts. However, there is case law in some places indicating that being in a stall puts you in a "private" space, not a public one.

The Internet

Internet hookups, which can be obtained on a variety of sites, must be done discreetly. Your profile should be as honest as possible while still making you look good. For example, don't put up a five-year-old picture of yourself and expect someone to be happy when your much-aged and 100-pound heavier self strolls up to the door. Lying is not sexy. If you're in your seventies, that's fine! Maybe there's a twenty-year-old gerontophiliac just waiting for your wrinkled testicles. Your game is only lost when you stop believing in it. However, it is also important to note that each site type has its own set of users and a certain personal ad style.

Chat sites—the name you choose is mostly useless, as is the bio chosen before entering your local chat room. Unless you have a fetish and require the cyber, master/servant, or similar rooms, choose the one closest to where you live. If you live in a large university town away from an urban area, the "[your state]

> Suggestion:
> Identifying as a top, is limiting, whereas "I like to top" is more flexible and realistic to the diversity of sexual tastes.

college" room almost exclusively houses people from your city (even if you don't go to school there). When entering the chat room, refrain from chatting in the main window. Only people who come on *every day* can do this without raising collective eyebrows. When you find an agreeable mate for the evening, open a private message starting with a cheesy greeting: "hey, what's up?" does wonders. They will almost invariably inform you that nothing is going on. You should then exchange pleasantries. After that, one party will ask the other "what are you into?" Don't be fooled; this is a thinly veiled way of asking whether you're a "top" or "bottom." Of course, we learned earlier that these are anal-focused and lame terms, so try to come up with an activity-based answer. If you are so unwise as to truthfully disclose your more interesting inclinations, they will likely respond "oh, cool," or, if some unacceptable habit has been disclosed, stop talking to you altogether.

Message boards and classified ads—the only people who use these services are straight, pretending to be straight, or have very specific needs. In other words: perfect for making new gay converts, but not much else. Proceed accordingly, but remember that many people read these while bored at work, so don't post too much identifying information.

Location-based chat services (on mobile devices)—these are great tools to make friends as well as lovers. In general, large cities have more sex-focused populations while smaller areas tend to be more chat-focused. Be sure to extend small talk for quite some time if you're visiting or living in a small area and want to meet a local. Otherwise, the experience and protocols are similar to chat-based Websites.

Drugs

While pursuing gay sexual escapades, you will at some point be offered drugs. While some take an all-or-nothing approach to chemical indulgences, it helps to know what you're getting into before ingesting. Here are some of the more common queer drugs and their relation to sex. Many of these are illegal and the law indicates you shouldn't do them, but since people do, it's best to be aware.

Poppers (usually legal, non-addictive)

Poppers are gay society's best-kept secret. They have been common in clubs, baths, and homes since the 1970s and have a very important use: they relax your muscles. A hit of poppers can make an asshole shockingly relaxed and receptive. For some people, they can increase hunger for sucking cock to unimaginable new heights. Outside of a sexual context, they'll probably just make you giggly, flushed, and a bit dizzy.

Technically, poppers are a variety of alkyl nitrates originally marketed as a cure for angina. Available as "VCR cleaner" or "leather cleaner" or a variety of other thoroughly unsuitable purposes, most sex shops carry them. They can make you lightheaded, but have no known long-term adverse effects. They're also non-addictive and legal in some places or "legal" where sold as cleaners, etc.

Crystal Meth (illegal, highly addictive, lots of side effects)

Crystal meth chemically provides the ability to dance for days and have as much sex as humanly possible without sleeping. While on meth you will think you are fabulous and you will be able to make loads of outrageously poor decisions in a row while thinking each is the *greatest idea you've ever had.* Oh yeah—it also rots your teeth out, is hugely addictive, and has loads of other life-altering negative side effects. They're bad news. Seriously.

Cocaine (illegal, addictive, lots of side effects)

You will think you're about to have sex with someone and they offer a bump. You think this means you'll be getting freaky soon, but you'll both likely end up talking about nothing in particular very quickly and then do more coke. It's fairly addictive, but most people can do a line once in a blue moon without serious side effects. It's very expensive and often cut with kerosene or ether.

Marijuana (legal in some places, psychologically addictive, some minor side effects)

Marijuana leads to endless make out sessions, lots of carbs, cuddling, and television watching. In the right setting, it can make dancing lots of fun. Some people find it relaxes them before sexual encounters. Heavy, long-term use effects memory, but infrequent use generally doesn't have profound effects other than adding "man" to the end of your sentences. No one has ever died of an overdose. Ever. In some countries and municipalities, marijuana is decriminalized or legal.

Ecstasy (illegal, possibly addictive, some side effects on as little as one dose)

Taking some ecstasy will make you love everyone and make all dance music the best ever. It makes every sensation intense and every moment wonderful. While on ecstasy you will rarely get hard, but you'll be cuddling and rubbing and who cares...I love you, guys. Frequent use can lead to malfunctioning serotonin in your brain.

Ketamine (not legal for humans, many side effects, possibly fatal)

Ketamine is a general anesthetic used by veterinarians and also a common club drug. At low doses, it produces vague feelings of being underwater—everything moves a little more strangely and fluidly. At high doses, it produces the state known as a "K hole." In a K hole, you're completely disassociated. Your brain and your body stop communicating properly and it can become impossible to do simple things like walk across a room or climb stairs. Some users report out of body experiences. Long-term users often experience memory loss.

GHB (illegal, many side effects, possibly fatal)

Although GHB is occasionally used as a date rape drug, it is a club drug staple. It is often compared to alcohol and ecstasy and makes dancing experiences more "sensual." Somewhat more telling, it is a pharmaceutical treatment for narcolepsy. Small amounts occur naturally in humans and most other animals. Every year at the major gay parties, someone overdoses on this. Mixing GHB with alcohol is what produces the typical "rape drug" scenario, blacking out, and/or loss of consciousness.

Sexual Politics

Navigating an Encounter with One Partner

One night, things will get hot and heavy and it'll be time to practice the art of gay sex. The chapter on getting laid in style describes in great detail how to bed people and what to do with them afterwards, this chapter focuses on the sex itself. Getting people in bed is an important skill, but once you get them there you better know what to do next. You probably won't date these one-off encounters, but *boy will you try*. If you want to get the sex you desire and not have word spread of your deeds and misdeeds, it's best to hone your encountering skills. Let's say, for example's sake, that you're drunk at a bar on a Friday night. You've been chatting with a hot gentleman for what seems like *hours* and it's time to seal the deal. But how? Work out the five following tools and you'll be on your way to better sexual encounters.

1) Whether or not

2) Where

3) What

4) Disclosures

5) In the middle of things (*In medias res*)

1) *Whether or not*: the first important thing to do is discover if it's going to happen at all. There are many ways to answer this question. If you've been making out and getting handsy, it may seem like you've got it in the bag. If you've just been chatting you might not really know even if all the signals give the go ahead. No matter how sure you are, you need to ask. Explicitly. If you are having a good time and shove his hand onto your rock hard cock,

you may be greeted with an unpleasant reaction. Then again, he may drop straight to his knees and get to work. It's impossible to be sure until you get permission. Obviously, the situation requires some finesse—telling someone how much you'd like to suck their cock is much more forward than a whispered, furtive, "want to take this somewhere more private?" Either way, be sure to ask and, if he says yes, proceed accordingly. If not, do inquire further, but don't get pushy. Aggressively pursuing a non-willing partner is sure to sour the mood. Just move on. If you're going to see one another again you can always give it a second try, but don't ask too many times. Even if he eventually succumbs to your advances, it's probably only a pity fuck on your behalf or because he has nothing better to do—it won't be fulfilling for either party.

2) *Where*: the next thing you need to figure out is where you will get together. Ask now before you get in a car or otherwise have awkward mid-trip geographical negotiations. If your house is a mess or you live with your mom then, by all means, go to his place. If neither of you has a space and he really is that hot, either get a hotel room or take him to a bathhouse with rooms. It may be weird to take a prospective trick to the baths, sure, but you can't beat a play space that costs thirty dollars or less and if he ends up being less than satisfactory you can always stick around and find a new partner.

3) *What*: the notion of what to do may seem intuitive to you, but your sense of "normal stuff" and his may be vastly different. Make sure to square up ideas of good times before getting to into it. Remember: *you are responsible for your own orgasm.* If you really like to get pissed on, suck toes, or engage in anything even remotely deviant that would pleasantly color the current sexual encounter, then ask about it before getting started. You can always say no and so can he, but if neither party tells their desires then they cannot be fulfilled. Simple as that. Figure out what you want (sucking/getting sucked, fucking/getting fucked, cuddling, kink, etc.) and figure out if he'll fill the need. If not, move on. There are plenty of horny gay men out there willing to give you what you need no matter how curious you may think it. Tap you inner filth: don't subvert your own desires just because "it's a nice thing to do" and maybe next time you'll get what you want. You will never ever get what you want if you don't ask for it. On the other hand, if

he asks for something new and you're not horrified or, better yet, turned on by the idea, then give it a try. You just might like it. Don't let mainstream fears of weirdness stop you—do what you want, try new things, and soon you'll find out your true desires.

4) *Disclosures:* if things look good and friskiness is about to commence and you have some condition or disease your partner should know about—TELL HIM. Now. Before you are in a situation where they're too aroused to make reasonable decisions (it's much harder to say no when a stiff cock is pressed to your asshole than while you're still talking about all the hideous things you plan to do to one another). There is no valid reason, ever, to not disclose any disease statuses before engagement. Hell, he might even be turned on by the idea—or at least not put off—so make sure to disclose and take all relevant precautions.

5) *In medias res*[2]: Sometimes, when you're in the middle of things, a new partner will do something you don't like. That's all right. It happens to everyone. When this happens, don't go through numerous minutes of fake-moan enjoyment with building anxiety. When someone is toothing your dick up and down, do yourself a favor and say, "please use less teeth." (or more!) It's really that easy. You shouldn't internalize this—rather, you should be confident enough in your filth to change course. Maybe they genuinely didn't notice. If they get pissed off and storm off from you "critiquing" their methods then good riddance! It would've been bad anyhow and you can always gossip with your friends about the outburst later.

If you get relevant permission (1), figure out where to go (2), figure out what to do (3), disclose relevant status issues (4), and accept some mild style alterations (5) then you'll be on your way to better, more positive, less hang-up-filled sexual encounters.

Navigating an Encounter with Two or More Partners

Fucking logistics. Seriously. Things get really tricky when trying to tango with more than two. Not only do you have to work out all

---

[2] Latin for "in the middle of things."

the necessary mono-play things, but, much like Website design, scalability gets tough as numbers increase. Problems that would never surface without extra people (who sucks which cock?) have immediate, session-ruining gravity. Multiple-partner sex requires great finesse and an even greater understanding of your own needs. When engaging in non-penetrative sexual events, things can be fairly fluid, but if anal happens, someone has to take it. Following are some intercourse-based group dilemmas you may run across and some strategies to avoid them.

All givers, no receivers—when everyone wants to fuck and no one wants to bottom you're all in trouble. The hoped-for solution is that one member takes it for the team. Another solution is to compete for it. Everyone engages in some form of competition like wrestling, rock paper scissors, strip poker, etc. and the loser gets fucked. This method only works when one or more people are at least a little uncomfortable being the receptive partner, but are into peer pressure. Sometimes guys just need a frame narrative to figure out which role to play that night. When trying to get a non-submitter to bottom, it sometimes helps to encourage power dynamics to eroticize the perceived-negative position of, ahem, reception.

All receivers, no givers—no one wants to top so the often joked-about bottom butt bumping commences. This is an easier fix since guys who enjoy the anal bottom position probably have toys laying around for when they need to "give" to themselves. Feel free to improvise ways to engage in mutual giving or, if you're really hardcore about it, invest in a double-headed dildo[3].

The clear problem in both role imbalances is that either the participants don't know what they like to give vs. receive, don't know how to ask for things, or no one is taking the "lead" to help when people get caught in an activity eddy and don't know what to do next. If you want to participate in orgiastic fun, please know what you like to give and what you like to receive. Top/bottom

---

[3] Be aware that sharing sex toys can be risky. If you're going to do something as reckless as sharing toys, make sure they are non-porous and that you properly sterilize them before and after. Using condoms on appropriately shaped instruments is also a healthy habit; it's probably easier to bring your own. Just in case.

dichotomies become quickly irrelevant since individual acts don't add up to an all-or-nothing stance: a bottom may like to suck cock (give) and enjoy a deep dicking (receive).

Thinking about the hanky code will probably help. The hanky code is a system in which gay men wear colored hankies in the back left or right pocket to indicate various sexual interests. They fall in and out of fashion regularly and are mostly used today by people looking for specific, hard-to-find activity partners. To get you thinking about what activities and positions you'd like to engage in, here are some example hankies used for common sexual exploits:

Yellow – Watersports – Left: piss on someone – Right: get pissed on

White – Masturbation – Left: get jerked off – Right: masturbate someone else

Light Blue – Oral Sex – Left: get head – Right: give head

Navy Blue – Anal Sex – Left: stick it in – Right: take it

Hunter Green – Daddy/Son – Left: daddy – Right: son

Lime – Food Play – Left: apply food – Right: wear food

Dark Pink – Tit Torture – Left: torturer – Right: tortured

Red – Fisting – Left: fister – Right: fistee

Magenta – Armpits – Left: get them licked – Right: lick them

Fuchsia – Spanking – Left: spank – Right: get spanked

Light Yellow – Spitting – Left: spit on Someone – Right: get spit on

Beige – Rimming – Left: get licked – Right: tongue flicking expert

Houndstooth – Biting – Left: biter – Right: bitten

Coral – Feet – Left: lick my feet – Right: foot licker

Light Pink – Dildos – Left: hold the dildo – Right: take the dildo

Teddy Bear – Cuddling – Left: big spoon – Right: little spoon

Car Keys – Location – Left: my place – Right: your place

Every gangbang needs a bottom and every piss party needs a toilet and the sooner you figure out whether you want to fill the pool or swim in it the more fun you will have in a group encounter. Know your hankies.

Navigating Multiple Fuck Buddies

If you plan to regularly sleep with a few different people—generally a more rewarding option than stranger-tricking, you need to remember three things: know your emotional limits, share your limits, and hold your limits. Knowing your limits means knowing how far you will physically and emotionally take the relationship with each person. Sharing your limits means expressing your expectations for your relationship even if it's "let's get together and fuck once a week: no more, no less." Holding your limits means not promising what you can't deliver (whether it's an activity, a commitment, exclusivity, etc.) If you are regularly bedding someone, even if that's all it is, you have responsibilities to one another.

First, figure out if any of them are datable. Are they? Well, maybe let them hang out for a while longer after encounters or do non-sexual things together. It's okay if sex is the only common ground as long as both parties know that's the way it is. While figuring out how close to get to the various people in your little black book, make sure and be open about others being involved. If you start to get cozy with one of the guys and he discovers you've been slutting it up with others after you cooed he was the only one, well, you deserve all that comes to you. Be honest. If they run off screaming after discovering you sleep with regular, multiple partners, then you probably weren't a good match.

Don't tell a guy you want to be exclusive when you don't. Don't tell a guy he's the only one when he's not. Don't say you're safe and clean if you aren't. If you engage in consistent dishonesty with regular partners, you don't deserve to have your dick looked at, let alone touched. Be straightforward, honest, and not a creep. If you have serious hang-ups about people knowing what you're up to then you shouldn't try anything even remotely emotionally dangerous—back to the tearoom with you, Mary.

Dating One Boy

Cheating is willfully breaking the rules. Changing the rules eliminates the need to cheat.

There are many, many books about dating and most of them are fine. Some examples are listed in Appendix A. There is no need to recount *ad nauseam* the many perils, pitfalls, and pleasures of dating. There are plenty of men out there and if he's no good, no matter how badly you want a boyfriend, follow the teachings of Dan Savage[4] and dump the motherfucker already (DTMFA). Here are some major dating mantras:

If you start dating a guy and he withholds sex in a way that makes you feel bad without feeling sexy then dump him. It is never, ever worth it. Regular, safe, interesting sex is one of the positives of dating someone.

If you are dating a man and he publicly freaks out every time you look at someone else and you don't get turned on by the admonishments then dump him. He is insecure and, if you stay and start apologizing, then so are you. Jealousy is not a sign of love.

If you are dating someone and he slaps, hits, belittles, or degrades you and it doesn't turn you or is not part of the negotiated activities then get the hell out. The abuse *will* get worse and your self-esteem can be ruined by the experience.

If you and your boyfriend regularly put down one another and intentionally try to make the other feel bad, and it isn't an agreed upon erotic practice, then break up or at least seek therapy. The process of intentionally making each other feel bad is called mutual invalidation. Relationships devolving into mutual invalidation are incredibly unhealthy and shockingly common for gays.

If you say you are exclusive with a man and you are not then you are a lying sack of shit. It is okay to date one boy and play with others as long as you and your partner discuss the mechanics. Maybe he wants to know when it happens. Maybe he doesn't. Maybe he wants you to recount your play sessions with other boys while fucking him. One thing nobody wants is a surprise STD when there is supposed exclusive commitment.

Dating can be awesome. Good, healthy relationships have many positive effects on your life and if it's your thing then, by all

---

[4] Dan Savage's weekly column "Savage Love" is available in your local city's weekly paper (the one that lists the cool stuff to do). It's also available online at http://www.thestranger.com/seattle/SavageLove.

means, do it. As it becomes increasingly accepted to be gay, the ability to find reasonably well-adjusted, dateable guys increases. Have fun, play safe, and take care of yourself.

Navigating Polyamorous Relationships

Sometimes one just isn't enough. You need more, you greedy pig. It's okay. Fortunately, polyamory comes in many forms. Sometimes you fuck on the side; sometimes you date on the side. If you are exclusive with more than one partner, you are engaging in polyfidelity. Your desire to play and date others is great as long as it's discussed and agreed upon by your primary partner. If you like to play around it is a really good idea to cultivate secondary boyfriends instead of tricking all willy-nilly. It's physically safer and generally leads to better sex. When dating multiple guys remember that, at the end of the day, you are responsible first to your primary relationship(s) and only second to your dick.

Dating numerous people requires massive amounts of communication. You need to discuss all the rules of dating others. Among other things, you need to work out the following:

When is it okay to see the other boyfriend? Daily? Weekly? Only when one partner is out of town?

Is there a sex act we should keep "between us"?

How should we mitigate disease risk with others?

Is it ever okay to sleep over at the other boyfriend's?

How much should you tell about adventures with other boyfriend?

As you work out answers to these questions others will arise and you will get a sense of what both you and your boyfriend are capable of handling. Make it clear to the other boyfriend what the borders are and that these are non-negotiable. There are some things that you should avoid doing or saying unless it arouses either partner:

Don't compare sexual habits, i.e. "my other boyfriend is so much better at sucking cock."

Don't compare penis sizes, especially if the three of you play together.

Leave some spaces free of one boyfriend or the other. Leave some place for the third party to go where he doesn't have to watch date time if he doesn't want to. In other words, don't regularly bring secondary boyfriend to your primary's favorite bar or restaurant.

Don't share the confidences of one boyfriend with another.

Don't bitch about one boyfriend with another.

Dating multiple people gets easier over time and much of the serious, soul-searching communication happens early in the relationship. After that you can get way more cock and ass than possible with one partner and some variety to keep all your relationships spicy.

Marriage

Some US states and some countries allow gay marriage and it has all the possibilities and pitfalls of normal marriage. It's okay to be wary of marriage—the most heteronormative establishment imaginable—and it is okay to get married. There are plenty of benefits to getting married—according to the US government there are thousands. Married couples get better deals for taxes, estates, property ownerships and transfers, monetary exchanges, immigration, and a host of other benefits. Go ahead and get hitched if that's your thing. The only case in which I strongly suggest getting married is if you plan to have or adopt kids. Otherwise, you have essentially no legal rights regarding the kid.

Remember, though, that many gay people have no plans to get married, get into domestic partnerships, or join in a civil union. The long arc of gay culture existed in spaces where marrying someone of the same gender was often not possible so over time gays have invented all sorts of interesting relationship dynamics. Before joining the ranks of the married, consider the cornucopia of bonding formations possible between one or more men.

Since there is fairly little precedent for gay weddings, it is part of your duty, should you choose to marry, to be hugely inventive with your vows and your reception. Especially your reception. This is the one party you will throw that all of your friends will remember for good or bad. There are two major things people remember about weddings: the food and the music. Make sure both are brilliant and you will have a party to remember.

Theatrical Fights: Keeping Your Claws Sharp

"Gay culture is the patriarchy turned in on itself."

--Dr. Matthew Callahan

Not all of gay life is tricks and treats. Eventually, you will have to fight someone, in public, and you best learn how to do it. Gay men love to dominate one another. As a result, occasions frequently arise where gays engage in highly public battles to continuously reinforce their social standing. No matter what your skills are, at some point you are going to have to defend yourself. That is what this chapter is about. There are numerous ways to rise to the top: a particularly strong jaw line, throwing out the washing machine because you actually use your abs as a washboard, keen wit, or using the tools of social psychology to manipulate those around you, but no matter your skills, at some point you're going to need to verbally spar.

The theatrical battle is as old as men doing men. Whenever two dudes decide to jockey for social positioning they engage in a battle of wits and style. The winner is generally the best rhetor and the most styled battler. While gay fights are predominantly verbal, in some locales they take the form of vogue—a complex dance-fight. There are many direct and indirect fighting styles that can be used, from the obvious to the sublime. There are attacks where the person knows they're being fought or where they wake up five years later in a cold sweat finally having realized what's been said. If dancing is the required fighting form then go out and rent *Paris Is Burning*, watch and mimic videos of people dancing online or otherwise train yourself. Keep vogue-battling with people of a similar skill level until you're a vogue black belt. Then dance your way into supremacy.

If verbal forms of combat are required, there is an assemblage of strategies perfect for asserting superiority. From the mild to the skewering, these varied approaches, if perfected, will win most all-verbal battles.

Reading

"You get in a smart crack and everyone laughs and kikis because you found a flaw and exaggerated it then you've got a good read going."

--Dorian Corey in *Paris Is Burning*

Reading is when you find the glamour that someone else is trying to diminish and you amplify it. Navigating the minefield of gay fighting in general requires a developed sense of glamour and divinity; one must be well tuned with one's inner self, and one's true strengths and weaknesses. If you are realistically aware of your shortcomings, you are less likely to miss the comments about them. Being hyper aware of others' glamour, also shows you where to poke and prod in conflict. Many reads deal with basic and obvious traits like hair, makeup, teeth, eyes, ears, face, outfit, tan, voice, masculinity|femininity, etc. To perform a read, simply choose something off about the person and crack a joke about it.

Say someone has crooked teeth and they're picking on you. To respond, try something like this read from the second season of RuPaul's Drag Race: "Was your barbeque cancelled? Because your grill is fucked." The first line looks like a traditional joke set up, with the insult being the punch line. Those skilled in camp are good readers because it follows the same paths. Mastering the two-line read is the essential first step before engaging in more elaborate reads.

The goal of reading is two-fold. The minor goal is to poke fun at the person. Unless the reader is seriously pissed, it is not appropriate to tackle the most vicious read topics: age, weight, and general competence. Instead, picking on something minor only lowers the read recipient's status slightly. Try to attend to the major goal of reading: humor. It is vastly more important to make yourself look fabulous for having a good read than to make the target look bad. Like so many gay arts, even fighting, making yourself look better gets you further than making others look worse. Make it *all about you.*

Reading is one of the few gay battle tools that can be used on friends and foes alike: friends for practice, of course, and enemies for the win. Beware when performing reads, though, as the target has a fair chance to retaliate afterwards. The only thing that halts the retaliation is to have everyone laugh. If the audience is laughing then they aren't paying attention to the rebuttal.

Viciousness: Mild

Obviousness: High, purposefully performative

Skill Level: Medium, high feedback rates make it, as it were, a quick read

Requires: Style, wit, delivery, knowledge of the other person

Winner Gets: Laughter and accolades

Loser Gets: An immediate chance to redeem himself

Use It On: Your friends, your peers, or anyone who needs to be knocked down a notch

Shade

"Shade is: I don't tell you you're ugly, but I don't have to tell you because you know you're ugly. And that's shade."

--Dorian Corey in *Paris is Burning*

You probably learned this from your mother. Remember, as a kid, when you were about to do something bad and your mom could stop you with a sideways glance? Those were your first lessons in shade. Shade is vastly more subtle and cruel than a read. A read, though insulting, is easy enough to fight back against and more light-hearted. Throwing shade cools the room ten degrees. The undisputed masters of throwing shade can ruin someone's reputation by raising an eyebrow. The process of shade is to pantomime or otherwise indicate that the shaded one is beneath contempt. It should become quickly obvious that the person throwing shade is calling the entire character of the shaded into question. The smallest and hardest form of shade is the disparaging look. If you already purse your lips, raise an eyebrow, theatrically sigh, or otherwise communicate destruction with a subtle expression then you probably have the foundations of throwing shade well in hand. Ultimately, shade is akin to jazz as described by Louis Armstrong, "Man, if you gotta ask, you'll never know."

In order to throw disparaging-look shade, focus your thoughts on all the details of the target's shortcomings. Now either purse your lips, raise an eyebrow, or both. If the target's failures are too insurmountable for silence, try adding a sour "hmm" in combination. You must feel the contempt for shade to work. If not, you will just look like you ate a lemon. If it's so bad you no longer wish to be in his presence, end the shade-throw by quickly and dramatically turning your head at least ninety degrees and walking away. If more emphasis is required, lead with your shoulder when turning away. Shade works in the opposite direction too. If you're normally very animated and you drop to a completely blank face, shake your head slightly, and casually walk away, you are throwing shade. There are more advanced and complex forms, but the basic one will get you far.

Ultimately remember that shade cannot be undone. Shade should not be seriously attempted amongst friends, as its degree of hostility is too high. If you're really mad, then by all means go ahead, but a sideways glance may be hard to take back. If you feel guilty after throwing shade, do not apologize. Your social standing will plummet.

Viciousness: High

Obviousness: Medium

Skill Level: Extreme

Requires: Mime and impression skills, reading skills

Winner Gets: Strong feeling of superiority

Loser Gets: A chill down his spine and increased insecurity

Use It On: Someone in an opposing peer group who makes your blood boil, someone you have no intention of becoming friends with

Underwhelming and False Compliments

"What a lovely outfit! Where did you get it, Lane Bryant?"

--Farrah Knight, drag queen

Sometimes you just need to keep a smile on your face. Maybe you have to be polite. Maybe a nasty look clashes with your outfit. Either way, at times rude remarks have to be kept subtle to prevent serious fights from breaking out. It's hard to escalate an impolite compliment because the tone is generally pleasant. Often the underwhelming compliment is used to keep from hurting people's feelings, such as what you might say to an actor in a bad play: "How did you memorize all those lines?"

To extend the theater metaphor, consider how Dr. Frank n Furter responds in *The Rocky Horror Show* after Janet completely misses his greeting of "enchanté" (due to her ignorance) and Frank purses his lips for a moment, composes himself, and continues: "*How nice*. And what charming underclothes you both have on. But here, put these [lab coats] on, they'll make you feel less…vulnerable." The "how nice" is generally said in the acidic method of the underwhelming compliment: the one complimenting judges the recipient and expresses it through tone of voice, but says something ostensibly polite. Ideally, the untrained receiver of a less-than-thrilled compliment doesn't notice at all and it's the audience that gets the joke, as it were.

This method works best either just before breaking off a conversation or in front of a group. If attempting this on an ally, make sure to over-emphasize the words to make it clear you're being funny and not overtly mean. If speaking to a frenemy or lower, all bets are off and either the underwhelming or false complimentary style can be used. To perform an underwhelming compliment, say extremely distant yet polite or bolstering yet clearly undeserved things. "Well, aren't you charming?" is a good first phrase. If you can say that and have the recipient be delighted while everyone around snickers, you have succeeded. When accomplished subtly, the attacked doesn't notice that he was insulted.

The false compliment is when you express a rude sentiment in a complimentary tone. This style doesn't provide the ego-protection of underwhelming compliments and is considerably more hostile. False compliments are similar to reads insofar as they often posses a set-up and a punch line. The execution is where the difference lies: the set up of a false compliment is a pleasant question or expression and the punch line is the mean part. Without the hook of niceness, the false compliment would lose all of its effectiveness and be, simply, bitchy. Being overtly bitchy is never, ever, charming, but skill in false compliments can transform common bitchiness to an art form.

Consider this section's epithet: "What a lovely outfit! Where did you get it, Lane Bryant?" The first sentence is said in an overtly positive, if saccharine, tone. The second starts off polite, but the store name is emphasized. Lane Bryant is a plus-size store so the speaker is calling you fat. Ouch. That's a false compliment. Gays from the Southeastern US, ever polite, are masters of this combat form, but often inverted, "She's got that lazy eye, but bless her heart for coming out tonight."

The defenses against the two strategies differ as well. To defend against an underwhelming compliment, when you're aware it is one, respond over-enthusiastically as though it's *the nicest thing you ever heard*. Forceful, positive enthusiasm is often sufficiently intimidating. The ultimate defense against any fashion-based false compliment is: "This old thing? It's vintage, darling. Where have you been?" This defense provides evidence that your taste is actually superior to the insulters and that you can identify prevailing styles outside of label-queendom. For all other cases, simply say "Oh, why, thank you" in the nastiest tone you can muster and move on. Compliment fighting is too absurd to be sustained. Best to use this strategy against itself and not shade.

Using shade after this or any sign you're upset shows that it worked. Remaining calm is essential.

Viciousness: Varies depending on how underwhelming it is and how clueless the recipient is.

Obviousness: Ideally none to recipient, completely obvious to everyone else

Skill Level: Mild, it's easy enough to figure out how to keep certain people from getting the joke

Requires: Knowledge of taste-based class hierarchies, delivery sufficient to alert onlookers to joke

Winner Gets: Fear and respect straight out of Machiavelli's *The Prince*

Loser Gets: Pariah status without knowing why

Use It On: People not worthy of your scene, those poor creatures

Drama-filled, All-out Bitchfests

All encounters have a "nuclear" option, and the bitchfest is the best bridge-burner in existence. It is only to be used in cases where a complete public whipping is required. The general strategy is to start with an affront-statement: "How *dare* you!" The initial volley must be at a high volume to engage as many onlookers as possible. After the initial audience-call, proceed to air the complete hideousness of the person in a logical, serial manner. Common excuses for bitchfests include: your boyfriend had unprotected sex with someone, caught something, and gave it you while pledging fidelity; someone was caught starting an especially vicious rumor; your now-ex boyfriend broke up with you in an unforgivable manner. Make sure to reveal the most embarrassing possible anecdotes about the person including: penis size, incriminating bad habits, cruising locales, addictions, and anything else they would only tell their most intimate companions.

Beware that screaming at someone at the top of your lungs in public makes you look highly unstable so this damages your image as well as the recipients. However, if it simply must be known that your roommate was charging high fashion ensembles to your credit card behind your back, quickly and quietly bankrupting you, then sometimes screaming your head off is the only logical step.

This method can only be employed, maximum, once every three years. Any more frequently and you will lose status while the victim of your tirade will seem positively sane and responsible by comparison. They will also have sufficient ammunition to start a smear campaign in retaliation. Bitchfests are considered a de-classing activity in some circles.

Viciousness: If they're not weeping in the fetal position afterwards you didn't try hard enough

Obviousness: Total, no one could possibly speak within a 100-foot radius while this is happening

Skill Level: Minimal, just be sure you're going to win the fight

Requires: Volume, a laundry list of complaints, ability to cry on command

Winner Gets: Highly public knowledge of what a loser so-and-so is

Loser Gets: To find a new place to hang out

Use It On: Someone you hope never sets foot where you are ever again; beware that if used improperly this method can backfire and make you look completely insane and, thus, a pariah

Rumors and Whisper Campaigns

Rumors and whisper campaigns are the silencer screwed onto your character assassination gun. They are quiet and sneak up on you before firing. Talking about people behind their backs, much like using silencers, is unsportsmanlike. Those who are rumored about have few ways to defend themselves and rumor-spreading is a cowardly act. If you find that rumor-spreading is your sole sensible course of action, never spread the following rumors: accusing someone of having HIV, accusing someone of a crime, or divulging or accusing someone of curious kinks. These do the most damage, it is never your business, and if you are discovered as the source, people will be *very* upset. If you find yourself a frequent rumor starter, it is best to try and do something more life affirming as the life of a falsifier is ultimately unfulfilling and reduces others' trust. Pick up knitting or something.

Rumors and whisper campaigns use the same communication channels as gossip, but are very different activities. Gossip is a bonding activity used between people to spread news through a social network—although it spreads scandal just as quickly. Rumors are a hack of the trust-based gossip network. The rumor-starter makes something up and passes it off as news. This person needs to have a high enough social standing to be believable, have the time and energy to seed numerous corners of a social network and when the story is believed it takes on a life of its own.

Social theory on gossip dictates that in order to gossip about someone you must be sufficiently integrated into the peer group and have high enough relative group standing to state your news. If nobody likes you, they will not trust your gossip. The best defense against a known rumor-spreader, then, is to identify him and reduce his trustworthiness. If he loses relative standing and is no longer credible, he will be incapable of further rumor-generation. People who start rumors often can't stop at one, so try and discover their other, ultimately heinous or untrue rumors. After making the discovery, when people mention the rumor explain that the guy who started it can't be believed for reason X. If enough people respond in this way, unsubstantiated boys who cry wolf will be rooted out.

Viciousness: Mild

Obviousness: Low, if well done, gossip is always quiet

Skill Level: Low, anyone and everyone can bitch about others

Requires: A juicy story about someone your peer group knows

Winner Gets: An increased reputation as a gossip, but this isn't necessarily a good thing

Loser Gets: Nasty things whispered behind their back

Use It On: The appropriate crowd for whom the story is about; don't go telling "between friends" gossip to relative strangers or your friends will get pissed when the news breaks

Battling Homophobia

Overcoming Your Own Homophobia

"Homophobia is the fear that other men will unmask us, emasculate us, reveal to us and the world that we do not measure up, that we are not real men. We are afraid to let other men see that fear. Fear makes us ashamed, because the recognition of fear in ourselves is proof to ourselves that we are not as manly as we pretend, that we are, like the young man in a poem by Yeats, 'one that ruffles in a manly pose for all his timid heart.' Our fear is the fear of humiliation. We are ashamed to be afraid."

--Michael S. Kimmel in *Masculinity as Homophobia*

"Masculine overcompensation is the idea that men who are insecure about their masculinity will behave in an extremely masculine way as compensation."

--Dr. Robb Willer

Far too often, gay men see themselves as damaged goods and find ways to drown their internalized homophobia. They drink too much, do too many drugs, or make some glamorous effort to go off the rails. Over the course of a lifetime, homophobic remarks and behaviors discourage gays. It's death by 1,000 cuts. In addition, sensitive and insecure gay men play into homophobic comments by *freaking the fuck out* when they are targets. Making fun of gay dudes is only fun when people over-react. Hateful words gain the most power when they consistently upset their targets. In order to effectively fight external sources of homophobia, you must first defeat your personal homophobia.

"But I'm out," you say, "How can I be a homophobe?" Easy. Do you make fun of gay guys more feminine than you? Do you feel like you are less of a man because you're gay? Are you incapable of sustaining healthy relationships? Do you consider yourself unlovable? These, among other indicators, suggest you still haven't dealt with that nagging feeling in the back of your head that, as a cock-smoking glamazon, you are somehow inferior. Fuck. That. Shit.

Some dudes are butch, some are femme, others switch back and forth, and still others live outside the gender binary all together. In order to fully accept your own homosexuality, it is critically important to accept that of others. Oftentimes, we project our self-critiques outward amplifying much of the self-hatred within the gay community. Pay attention, when having it out with other gays, about exactly *what* offends you—it just may be something you strongly dislike about yourself.

As a gay man, you are no longer expected to confirm to hegemonic gender norms, nor should you try. As Michael Kimmel succinctly puts it: "this…is the great secret of American manhood: *We are afraid of other men.* Homophobia is a central organizing principle of our cultural definition of manhood." Gay-baiting, saying "no homo" and calling people faggots are the most common ways to call in the gender police. By constantly reinforcing that anything even remotely feminine or dude-cuddly makes you a faggot, masculinity is enforced. Invisible borders are drawn around sensitivity, grace, and high-heeled shoes. However, by *being* a faggot, the argument is moot. If the most common refutation of manliness is calling someone a faggot and you *are* a faggot, then this hate mongering should entirely lose its power over you. But it doesn't.

Gay men bristle and feel less-than when men call each other faggots when what they should be saying is "Yes. And?" Every single non-masculine thing you could ever do in your entire life— crying, swishing, performing, decorating well, having taste, being able to dance, dressing nicely—is already contained in the identifying word. It should be well beyond worry that you're gay. Consider the alternative: the *most* masculine man shows no emotion, walks stiffly, dresses plainly, decorates poorly, eats blandly, has terrible taste, and doesn't dance. Who the fuck wants to live without any of those things? Terrified of showing emotion or being in touch with your feelings? Ugh. You don't have to sit for tea and sympathy with your best friends, but being aware of your feelings—even if they aren't laid out for public display—is a hallmark of being well adjusted.

Further, conventional and stereotypical masculinity is associated with the working class and being a "sissy" is a solid mark of prepdom. Though ends of the spectrum are equally valid and thoroughly play-acted by gays—and it's perfectly acceptable to be both rich and not-so-much—remember that asserting consistent masculine values is a declassing activity. Calling the gender police is also calling the class police: don't be so déclassé. Indeed, realize that norm enforcement is a giant game of fear-mongering and status anxiety and that, by being a faggot, you should be well on your way to overcoming both. Whether presenting as a he-man or sassy-man you are still a man.

Dealing with External Homophobia

Research shows that straight men, when their masculinity is threatened, behave in a variety of ways: they become more aggressive and more likely to engage in homo-hating behaviors. Thus, threatening a straight guy's masculinity by calling him a faggot makes him want to call other guys faggots and the cycle goes ever onward. Thus, when someone calls you a faggot, it is not in your best interest to get in his face and say "Who you calling faggot, breeder?" This threat to his masculinity will only increase future homophobic instincts. Instead, you should try and break the cycle in one of three main ways: ignore it, hit on him[5], or call him out. After mastering these three methods feel free to develop your own and share it with friends and allies.

Ignore It

One of the most difficult, yet most effective ways to respond to written and verbal name-calling is to ignore it. This is a perfect

---

[5] This strategy is dangerous and can backfire badly enough that you can end up in the hospital or worse. I've seen it work swimmingly in capable hands, but only the talented or intimidating can pull it off without escalating conflict.

time to employ shade. Tell this person they are below contempt. Stare directly in their eyes, nod your head a bit, and walk away. Don't get too sassy about your shade here or you will look ruffled. This method is not very much fun, nor good for stories, but it thoroughly gets the job done. If someone calls you a faggot and you simply ignore it, you break the cycle by taking away the power of masculinity-diminishment. Being called a faggot just doesn't seem like much of a threat when you, ya know, are one. So, let it be. The guy's friends, if they're any use at all, will eventually become embarrassed for him if he keeps it up and will hopefully shush him. Since his calling-out of you was ineffective, that lowers his ability to de-masculinize others and thus inadvertently lowers his feelings of masculinity, but raises yours.

Hit on Him

To a straight man running around shouting sexual epithets, few things are more horrifying than realizing anti-gay language brings immediate, highly public, flirtation. This method only works in situations where shaming is possible, but it can stop a dude dead in his tracks[6]. As soon as the guy starts getting aggressive at you appear physically aroused and start cooing. When the dude realizes his attempt at intimidation is instead an act of gay-arousal he will probably stop pretty quickly. This totally short-circuits the acting-tough-means-being-straight feedback loop and in as few as three volleys, he should be running with his tail between his legs.

Note: if the guy looks like he might be carrying a weapon or shaming is not possible (or if you're by yourself in relative isolation) this is not a good course of action. This strategy can be dangerous.

Call Him Out

"The lady doth protest too much, methinks."

--Hamlet

Fun fact: during the first decade of the 2000s, numerous high-profile homophobes have been caught engaging in gay sex. Larry

---

[6] Or, if handled improperly, it can escalate the situation and get you injured. Seriously. Don't try this at home.

Craig tapped his feet; George Rekers, founder of the anti-gay Family Research Council and former officer of the National Association for Research & Therapy of Homosexuality, hired a rent boy to carry his luggage, etc. This is an easy fact to use to your advantage. Make a public note that intensely homophobic people are often raging against their *own* gay feelings. If outspoken homophobia is re-branded as an outpouring of internalized homophobia, then average douche bags will think twice before claiming a little too loudly about their disgust/interest in other's cock-sucking habits.

There is also a less degrading method: the fast and fierce education. Make it known that it is not okay to call you a faggot and you will not be intimidated. This double-shot—preferably verbal and not physical—will often stop an aggressor.

Gay Bashing

Sometimes people are not looking to hurt your feelings; they are looking to hurt your body. If you see someone coming at you looking to fuck you up there is only one suitable course of action: get the hell out of there and call the cops. If you are properly trained you can fight back, but a pissed off homo-hater armed with a baseball bat is not to be trifled with.

Apocryphal Strategies

When being harassed while you are in a group, form into a phalanx and snap your fingers while simultaneously taking a step forward. The more choreographed it looks, the creepier it is.

When someone says something is "gay" meaning "bad" say: "no, *this* is gay" and proceed to do something over-the-top queer. It reframes the conversation towards a less hostile meaning of gay.

Sometimes it helps to just act crazy. Crazy beats angry like paper beats rock—it doesn't make sense, but totally works. For example: if someone throws food at you pretend it is the greatest gift ever and excitedly rub it all over your body. This is when your skills in camp will get you out of a situation.

People Who Should Be Given No Quarter

Most people who engage in nasty name-calling have a chance at reform and should be admonished. Everyone can and should have a chance at redemption, except the following people. These are the self-hating scum of the Earth: the closet cases in positions of power who ruin the lives of other gays. The following people, when engaging in homophobic behaviors and known to be gay, should be immediately outed:

> Politicians who support anti-gay legislation

> Religious officials running institutions trying to pray the gay away

> Anyone involved in producing national-level anti-gay media messages

If you are their stripper, trick, secret lover, or escort, *do not whip your dick out for these men.* Until they come clean and earn it, they should be given no warmth. This homophobia is the most destructive because it's a tireless effort to destroy the queer inside himself on a massive scale. Out these fuckers until it becomes clear that propagating highly public messages of gay hatred implies that you are gay.

The Performance of Gender

In daily life, we have many masks for many occasions both masculine and feminine. There are a wide variety of reasons and contexts where it is okay or not okay to behave in certain ways and no one should make you feel guilty about your "performed" gender. For example, it is all right to behave in an intentionally butch manner at work and then get all "Hey, Mary" when out at the bar. It's better if you can present the face you want all the time, but there are plenty of occasions where one might want to slip under the radar. Realize that both masculine and feminine behaviors are theatrical masks. It is, for example, not considered appropriate to dance around complimenting the hair of everyone at the corporate board meeting—or maybe it is at company awesome. The ability to project varied genders is one of the greatest assets of being gay so you may as well learn to do it. If, for whatever reason, you are extremely masculine or feminine in manner and appearance and incapable of shifting, then you will, in time, develop an extensive set of mechanisms to guide you through times when it would be so much easier to shift. Don't stress it if you're a 6'8", muscled, big-dicked sensitive artist or a nellie business executive: everyone gets upset with their own situation now and again and practicing varied gender presentations helps phase shifts.

Everyone has reasons for their gender expressions and fuck you if you disagree. Seriously. Don't belittle others because they are "too femme" or "not gay enough." It's so much more fun to compliment each other on lovely outfits and life choices and come up with escalating, if outrageous, compliments. "Well, aren't you just divine?"

Gathering Recruits

"As a mother, I know that homosexuals cannot biologically reproduce children; therefore, they must recruit our children."

--Anita Bryant

Converting Straight Men

If, when you get old, you want some hot young orderly to bend over and change your bedpan then it is essential new gays be recruited. This task isn't as easy as it seems. For decades, heteros have been spreading the most awful rumors claiming we have endless fantasies about getting hot young jocks and convincing them it's okay—nay preferable—to be gay. Naturally, it's true. Thankfully, it's growing less fashionable to hate faggots so straight dudes can exist in deliciously fluid sexual categories like "mostly heterosexual" or "hetero-flexible." Thus, it is even more challenging to identify as gay and thus all gay men should follow these methods to helping newly unleashed recruits acclimate.

Helping the Newly Out

Everybody comes out at some point. When they do, they are as vulnerable and pliable as you were when you began the journey to fabulous you're now completing. Now that you have completed your transition and spread your wings it is time for you help the newly out. Remember that nice guy at the bar who introduced you around? How about the first guy who blew you and smiled at all your beginner's mistakes? Yes, well, it is now your turn to extend this courtesy to others.

Each gay person, upon coming out, feels they discovered a magical wonderland full of alien rules and customs. Having been around the block, as it were, the seasoned gays realize that they had predecessors and will have replacements and it is your responsibility to provide the three following services (aside from physical services, of course): tell them where stuff is, let them know they have a history, and provide some charity.

Tell Them Where Stuff Is

Among the first things a newly out gay needs is a set of signifiers and a place to wear them. Tell the poor young queers where to get a gay haircut, some gay coffee, a gay breakfast, and a gay cocktail. Tell them where the right neighborhood is and which bars they might like in it. Give them the lay of the land and, no matter how foolish the questions, let them know that you too were once a greenhorn and not the impeccable creature now standing before them. Make it seem fabulous enough and you might even get a date out of it.

Let Them Know They Have a History

While constructing a queer ego and identity a new recruit may make the common mistake of thinking they're the first person to *ever* dress in drag, behave like a gender outlaw, listen to a certain band, wear a particular color combination, or revive a previous decade's clothing in a fresh and enticing way. They might think their little band of glorious, fresh-faced members of the queer counter public are special. They may be special, but they're not the first. You know it, I know it, and deep down they know it, but hope it isn't true. Let them know that there have been others like them for a long time and that there are/were gay icons other than Lady Gaga, Cher, and Madonna. Some of them are even men! A young gay man thinks his love of current pop music is original and insightful. It is not. A young gay man thinks that listening to the music from Into the Woods makes him the gayest man alive. Again, not true. Please, let the children know of Erasure, Cole Porter, Allen Ginsberg, Oscar Wilde, and all the fantastic faggot art and culture of yesteryear. They'll thank you later. Let them know of the great exploits of elder faggots you may know or that you've heard about who bravely acted "out" at a time when that may have meant a prison sentence or worse. Remember: schools try their best to never mention the word gay out loud so it is our job to convey our history.

Provide Some Charity

If we're going to function as a tribe, we have got to work together. There are loads of gay community groups, both local and national, that can use your dollars and your efforts. If you truly don't feel represented by the current offerings then start new clubs, groups, events, or charities. Even if it's a once a year thing, tithe to important LGBT charities or spent an afternoon now and again volunteering for a queer non-profit. If there is any meaning to the word "community," this is it. Otherwise, our sexuality and unique perspectives on the world mean nothing, represent nothing, promote nothing. We already have the neighborhoods and the neighbors so please pledge to help those who don't or can't live out, safely, 24/7. It's everyone's responsibility to make life better for all the queers—the butch, the femme, and everything in between.

Wrap It Up, Mary

"You're going to meet the most extraordinary men, the sexiest, brightest, funniest men, and you're going to fall in love with so many of them, and you won't know until the end of your life who your greatest friends were or your greatest love was."

--Harvey Milk in *Milk*

Now that you've been out for some time you are undoubtedly fabulous. It's true. After a few years of work, you have gathered the requisite skills required to succeed in the grand kingdom of queers. As time passes, you will meet more wonderful people than you knew possible and realize the benefits of living in the Fraternal Alliance of Gays. As a journeyman gay and from here on out, it is your responsibility to live your everyday as out as possible. Even though there are struggles to come, realize that it gets better each day. Remember what an awkward lad you once were? Remember that distinctive feeling of isolation before you came out? We all feel like we're alone and that no one feels the way we do, but we're not alone at all.

There is a massive, networked, supportive gay community everywhere you go. It may be small, but it exists. A friend of mine once missed a train connection and was stranded overnight in a town where he knew no one. He found the local gay bar and showed up suitcase in hand. He met a perfectly friendly fellow there who set him up in his extra bedroom. Another friend of mine was having trouble with airline ticketing. The first clerk was quite nasty. A gay clerk, seeing the situation, came up and told his rude co-worker to go to lunch. The gay clerk fixed the problem and bumped him to first class as well. Make your motto: "We're here, we're queer, and we provide each other with assistance."

A friend of mine told me that, back in the 1960s, he used to buy Physique Pictorial at the drug store in his small California hometown, terrified though he was that he would immediately be outed. He wasn't. Instead, he got to understand his erotic feelings because of Los Angeles queers brave enough to take nearly-nude pictures of men when it was illegal. The fraternity is real.

Find your neighboring gays and meet up for coffee, movies, or something sinister. Even if you're not meant to be friends forever you will appreciate knowing that someone in your town experiences similar things—both good and not-so-much. No matter who you are or what you're into—sexually and otherwise, gay peers exist. Let's remember our gay forefathers, some of whom risked it all to promote a queer view of the world. Thanks to the Stonewall rioters, the Mattachine Society, the Daughters of Bilitus, the Sisters of Perpetual Indulgence, The Imperial Court System, ACT UP, twentieth century physique photography magazines, queer musicians, artists, authors, activists, and men and women brave enough to act like faggots and dykes in public so we can have the glorious gay society of today and tomorrow.

As we continually learn to love ourselves as individuals and as a tribe the glory of gay will only increase. Be yourself. Be out. Be fabulous. Take care.

Appendix A

Resource Lists

The following lists are by no means a comprehensive list of all queer culture. However, a canon certainly does exist, changes over time, and is an important facet of growing into a well-rounded homosexual. Many gay books reference one another in the introductions so starting with one will take you to others. Not all of the bands, movies, or books are gay. Indeed, some are made by enlightened straights yet profoundly resonated in queer circles. Some entries are current and some are retro, but if you want to master the culture you should read, watch, and listen to them all.

If You Are in Danger or Suicidal

1. The Trevor Project (youth). 1-866-488-7386. www.thetrevorproject.org

2. The Gay and Lesbian National Hotline (adults). 1-888-843-4564.

3. The Nineline (for homeless and runaway youth). 1-800-999-9999.

4. The Hotline (national domestic violence hotline). 1-800-799-7233.

5. *Hello Cruel World: 101 Alternatives to Suicide for Teens, Freaks, and Other Outlaws* by Kate Bornstein

Coming Out Resources

1. *The Real World Guide to Coming Out* by Steven Petrow

2. *Am I Blue? Coming Out from the Silence* by Marion Dane Bauer

3. *It Gets Better: Coming Out, Overcoming Bullying, and Creating a Life Worth Living* edited by Dan Savage

4. *The Velvet Rage: Overcoming the Pain of Growing Up Gay in a Straight Man's World* by Alan Downs

5. *The Homo Handbook: Getting in Touch with Your Inner Homo: A Survival Guide for Lesbians and Gay Men* by Judy Carter

Gay Dating Books (If You're Dating One Person)

1. *Dynamic Duos* by Keith W. Swain

2. *Keeping Mr. Right: The Gay Man's Guide to Lasting Relationships* by Kenneth George

3. *Love Between Men: Enhancing Intimacy and Resolving Conflicts in Gay Relationships* by Rik Isensee

4. *The Mandates: 25 Real Rules for Successful Gay Dating* by Dave Singleton

5. *Against Love: A Polemic* by Laura Kipnis

Required Anti-assimilationist Reading

1. *That's Revolting!: Queer Strategies for Resisting Assimilation* by Mattilda Bernstein Sycamore

2. *Nobody Passes: Rejecting the Rules of Gender and Conformity* by Mattilda Bernstein Sycamore

3. *Gender Outlaw: On Men, Women, and the Rest of Us* by Kate Bornstein

4. *The Trouble with Normal: Sex, Politics, and the Ethics of Queer Life* by Michael Warner

5. *Public Sex: The Culture of Radical Sex* by Pat Califia

Great Gay Coming of Age Books

1. *How I Learned to Snap: A Small Town Coming-of-age and Coming-out Story* by Kirk Read

2. *Gutterboys* by Alvin Orloff

3. *A Boys Own Story/The Beautiful Room Is Empty* by Edmund White

4. *The Mysteries of Pittsburgh* by Michael Chabon

5. *Running with Scissors: A Memoir* by Augusten Burroughs

Other Gay Handbooks

1. *The Homosexual Handbook* by Angel d'Archangelo

2. *The Gay Insider: A Hunter's Guide to New York and Thesaurus of Phallic Lore* by John Francis Hunter

3. *The Butch Manual* by Clark Henley

4. *The Unofficial Gay Manual* by Kevin DiLallo

5. *The Bear Handbook: A Comprehensive Guide for Those Who Are Husky, Hairy, and Homosexual, and Those Who Love 'Em* by Ray Kampf

Gay History (Non-Fiction)

1. *Gay New York: Gender, Urban Culture, and the Making of the Gay Male World, 1890-1940* by George Chauncey

2. *Wide Open Town: A History of Queer San Francisco* by Nan Alamilla Boyd

3. *Gay L.A.: A History of Sexual Outlaws, Power Politics, and Lipstick Lesbians* by Lillian Faderman

4. *The History of Sexuality* by Michel Foucault

5. *Times Square Red/Times Square Blue* by Samuel R. Delaney

Required Gay Reading (Because I Said So)

1. *How Long Has This Been Going On?* by Ethan Mordden

2. *Dancer from the Dance* by Andrew Holleran

3. *Queer* by William S. Burroughs

4.   *Brokeback Mountain* by Annie Proulx

5.   *A Single Man* by Christopher Isherwood

6.   *The Portrait of Dorian Gray* by Oscar Wilde

7.   *Shock Value/Crackpot/Role Models* by John Waters

8.   *Disco Bloodbath* by James St. James

9.   *Homos* by Leo Bersani

10.   *A Confederacy of Dunces* by John Kennedy Toole

Required Kinkster Reading

1.   *The Ethical Slut: A Practical Guide to Polyamory, Open Relationships, and Other Adventures* by Dossie Easton

2.   *Tea Room Trade: Impersonal Sex in Public Places* by Laud Humphreys

3.   *Faeries, Bears, and Leathermen: Men in Community Queering the Masculine* by Peter Hennen

4.   *The 120 Days of Sodom, or the School of Libertinism* by the Marquis de Sade

5.   *Venus in Furs* by Leopold von Sacher-Masoch

6.   *SM 101: A Realistic Introduction* by Jay Wiseman

Totally Fucked Up Gay Books

1.   *Exquisite Corpse* by Poppy Z. Brite

2.   *Mysterious Skin* by Scott Heim

3.   *Ragazzi di Vita* by Pier Paolo Passolini

4.   *Death in Venice* by Thomas Mann

5.   *Fag Hag* by Rod Rodi

The Gay Agenda

When the religious right refers to the "gay agenda" these are the texts they quote. These are essentially a PR campaign designed in the early 1990s. If you read these books and pay attention to the history of past few decades it will become clear that these books were right on target. Everything pretty much happened the way it was outlined in 1990.

1. *After the Ball: How America Will Conquer Its Fear and Hatred of Gays in the 90s* by Marshall Kirk and Hunter Madsen

2. *The Overhauling of Straight America* by Marshall K. Kirk and Erastes Pill

Twenty Five Queer/Queer-Culturally-Significant Singers and Bands (years active)

1. Judy Garland (1924-1969)

2. Cher (1963-present)

3. David Bowie (1964-present)

4. Judas Priest (1968-present)

5. ABBA (1972-1982)

6. Sylvester (1972-1987)

7. Patrick Cowley (1976-1982)

8. The B-52s (1976-present)

9. The Village People (1977-present)

10. Madonna (1979-present)

11. Dead or Alive (1980-present)

12. Pet Shop Boys (1981-present)

13. Divine (1982-1988)

14. Bronski Beat (1983-1995)

15. Erasure (1985-present)

16. RuPaul (1985-present)

17. Army of Lovers (1987-2001)

18. The Magnetic Fields (1989-present)

19. Pansy Division (1991-present)

20. Rufus Wainwright (1993-present)

21. Placebo (1994-present)

22. Johnny McGovern (1998-present)

23. Cazwell (2000-present)

24. The Scissor Sisters (2001-present)

25. Lady Gaga (2005-present)

Twenty-five Fabulous Gay Films (Country, Release Year)

There is a common film trope known colloquially as "bury your gays." It's a phenomenon, especially in older films, in which any obviously gay character must either die or be otherwise punished for his "wicked" ways. Although I was moved when it happened in *Rebel without a Cause*, I generally find it an abhorrent way to portray gays and try to avoid it here as best as possible.

1. *Pink Flamingoes* (US, 1972)

2. *The Naked Civil Servant* (UK, 1975)

3. *La Cage Aux Folles* (France, 1978)/*The Birdcage* (US, 1996)

4. *Parting Glances* (US, 1986)

5. *Maurice* (UK, 1987)

6. *Torch Song Trilogy* (US, 1988)

7. *Paris Is Burning* (US, 1991)

8. *The Teen Apocalypse Trilogy:*

   a. *Totally Fucked Up* (US, 1993)

   b. *The Doom Generation* (US, 1995)

   c. *Nowhere* (US, 1997)

9. *The Adventures of Priscilla, Queen of the Desert* (Australia, 1994)

10. *To Wong Foo, Thanks for Everything, Julie Newmar* (US, 1995)

11. *Beautiful Thing* (UK, 1996)

12. *Edge of Seventeen* (US, 1998)

13. *Get Real* (UK, 1999)

14. *Trick* (US, 1999)

15. *But I'm a Cheerleader* (US, 2000)

16. *Sordid Lives* (US, 2000)

17. *L.I.E.* (US, 2001)

18. *Die, Mommie, Die!* (US, 2003)

19. *Girls Will Be Girls* (US, 2003)

20. *Mambo Italiano* (Canada, 2003)

21. *Mysterious Skin* (US, 2004)

22. *Brokeback Mountain* (US, 2005)

23. *Gay Sex in the 70s* (US, 2005)

24. *Another Gay Movie* (US, 2006)

25. *Were the World Mine* (US, 2008)

A Few Camp Classics (Country, Release Year)

1. *Whatever Happened to Baby Jane?* (US, 1962)

2. *Faster Pussycat! Kill! Kill!* (US, 1965)

3. *Grey Gardens* (US, 1975)

4. *The Rocky Horror Picture Show* (US, 1975)

5. *Mommie Dearest* (US, 1981)

Twenty-five Fabulous Gay People (Occupation, Birth/Death Dates)

1. Oscar Wilde (writer, playwright, 1854-1900)

2. Marcel Proust (writer, 1871-1922)

3. Jean Cocteau (writer, playwright, filmmaker, 1889-1963)

4. Langston Hughes (poet, 1902-1967)

5. Christopher Isherwood (writer, 1904-1986)

6. Tennessee Williams (playwright, 1911-1983)

7. William S. Burroughs (writer, 1914-1997)

8. Tom of Finland (artist, pornographer, 1920-1991)

9. Bob Mizer (photographer, filmmaker, pornographer, 1922-1992)

10. Jose Sarria (drag queen, activist, founder of the Imperial Court System, 1922-)

11. Gore Vidal (writer, playwright, 1925-)

12. Michel Foucault (philosopher, 1926-1984)

13. Allen Ginsberg (poet, 1926-1997)

14. Andy Warhol (artist, 1928-1987)

15. Harvey Milk (politician, 1930-1978)

16. Larry Kramer (writer, activist, 1935-)

17. Sir Ian McKellen (actor, 1939-)

18. Robert Mapplethorpe (photographer, 1946-1989)

19. John Waters (filmmaker, writer, art critic, 1946-)

20. Sir Elton John (singer, 1947-)

21. Harvey Fierstein (actor, playwright, 1952-)

22. Charles Busch (playwright, actor, drag queen, 1954-)

23. Michael Musto (writer, socialite, pundit, 1955-)

24. Chi Chi Larue (drag queen, pornographer, DJ, 1959-)

25. Dan Savage (writer, political pundit, 1964-)

Ten Important Drag Queens

1. RuPaul (New York)

2.   Jackie Beat (Los Angeles)

3.   Lady Bunny (New York)

4.   Hedda Lettuce (New York)

5.   Miss Coco Peru (New York)

6.   Peaches Christ (San Francisco)

7.   Hecklina (San Francisco)

8.   Anna Conda (San Francisco)

9.   Christeene Vail (Austin, Texas)

10.   Sherry Vine (New York)

Ten Queer Plays and Musicals (Most Are Also Movies)

1.   *The Rocky Horror Show*

2.   *Rent*

3.   *Avenue Q*

4.   *Angels in America*

5.   *Love! Valour! Compassion!*

6.   *Hedwig and the Angry Inch*

7.   *Pearls Over Shanghai*

8.   *Victor/Victoria*

9.   *The Adventures of Priscilla, Queen of the Desert*

10.   *Psycho Beach Party*